TELL ME WHO I AM

TELL ME WHO I AM

*James Agee's Search
for Selfhood*

Mark A. Doty

Louisiana State University Press
Baton Rouge and London

Copyright © 1981 by Louisiana State University Press
All rights reserved
Manufactured in the United States of America

Designer: Patricia Douglas Crowder
Typeface: VIP Garamond
Typesetter: G & S Typesetters, Inc.
Printer: Thomson-Shore, Inc.
Binder: John Dekker & Sons, Inc.

LIBRARY OF CONGRESS CATALOGING IN PUBLICATION DATA

Doty, Mark.
  Tell me who I am.

  Bibliography: p.
  Includes index.
  1. Agee, James, 1909–1955. 2. Authors,
American—20th century—Biography. I. Title.
PS3501.G35Z62 818'.5209 [B] 80-22440
ISBN 0-8071-0758-1

The author wishes to express his gratitude for permission to quote from the following copyrighted material:

From *A Death in the Family* by James Agee, copyright © by the James Agee Trust. Used by permission of Grosset and Dunlap, Inc. Published in Britain by Peter Owen, London.

From *Let Us Now Praise Famous Men* by James Agee, published by Houghton Mifflin Company. Copyright © 1939 and 1940 by James Agee. Reprinted by permission of the publisher. Published in Britain by Peter Owen, London.

From *Letters of James Agee to Father Flye*, Second Edition by James Agee, published by Houghton Mifflin Company. Copyright © 1962 by James Harold Flye and the James Agee Trust. Copyright © 1971 by James Harold Flye. Reprinted by permission of the publisher. Published in Britain by Peter Owen, London.

From *The Morning Watch* by James Agee, published by Houghton Mifflin Company. Copyright © 1950 by James Agee. Reprinted by permission of the publisher. Published in Britain by Peter Owen, London.

From *The Collected Short Prose of James Agee*, edited by Robert Fitzgerald, published by Houghton Mifflin Company. Copyright © 1968, 1969 by the James Agee Trust. Copyright © 1968 by Robert Fitzgerald. Reprinted by permission of the publisher. Published in Britain by John Calder (Publishers) Ltd.

From *The Collected Poems of James Agee*, published by Houghton Mifflin Company. Copyright © 1962, 1968 by the James Agee Trust. Reprinted by permission of the publisher. Published in Britain by John Calder (Publishers) Ltd.

From James H. Flye, "An Article of Faith," and Robert Saudek, "J. R. Agee, '32: A Snapshot Album, 1928–1932," published in the *Harvard Advocate*, CV (February, 1972).

For my parents,
James Edward Doty
&
Merciel Smith Doty,
whose searches for selfhood have
taught me to seek my own selfhood
with compassion, love, and mirth

CONTENTS

ACKNOWLEDGMENTS

I should like to thank Professors James Ackerman, Gates Agnew, and Roy Battenhouse of Indiana University for the roles they played in helping to shape and define the manuscript. Professor James Justus has my particular thanks and gratitude for perceptive criticism and scholarly encouragement.

I am indebted to the following individuals who so willingly allowed me to interview them about their personal relationships with James Agee: Father James Harold Flye, for his deep interest in this treatment of his former pupil and for his faithful correspondence; Mrs. Emma Agee Ling, Agee's sister; Mr. Dwight Macdonald, journalist and close friend of the writer, who thoughtfully loaned me his correspondence with Agee; Mr. David McDowell, the writer's editor and intimate friend for his generosity as executor of the James Agee Trust; Mrs. Clyde Medford and Mrs. Ann Tate, Agee family friends; Miss Paula Tyler, the writer's aunt; and Mrs. Olivia Wood, Mrs. Alma Neuman, and Mrs. Mia Agee, for their warmth, graciousness, and openness.

I am grateful to William Morrow and Company, publishers of *The Restless Journey of James Agee* by Genevieve Moreau, for their kind permission to quote from that work.

My research has also been aided by the kind help that Dr. Robert Coles, Mr. Tad Mosel, and Mr. Roswell Spears III afforded in helping

ACKNOWLEDGMENTS

to draw a composite portrait of the writer through letters, telephone conversations, and interviews. Mrs. Jeannie A. Gooch and the staff of the James Agee Memorial Library, Saint Andrews, Tennessee; Ms. Ellen S. Dunlap and the staff of the Humanities Research Center, the University of Texas at Austin; and the Office of Research and Development, Indiana University, all offered invaluable assistance in my research.

As the work approaches completion, I continue to be grateful for the indexing and proofreading skills of Mrs. Clinton R. Harris, graciously offered and competently employed. To Ms. Judy Bailey, Louisiana State University Press editor, my profound thanks for bringing to the manuscript a renewed sense of stylistic precision and clarity of line.

Finally, I wish to recognize four individuals whose affirmation during this project—and before—have made me deeply grateful. The Reverend A. Hardy Nall, Jr., has been a true and generous friend. I shall always be appreciative of his interest, guidance, and desire to challenge me as a person. Sarajane Blythe Doty, my wife and dearest friend, has shared with me in this project from its inception. For her love, devotion, and sacrifice and for enabling—more than anyone else—this manuscript to become a reality, I owe the most profound debt. To my parents, Dr. and Mrs. James E. Doty, for their lifetime of creative nurture, wisdom, and authentic care, this work is appreciatively dedicated.

INTRODUCTION

Jim . . . complicated his creative life so much that he was
rarely able to come to simple fulfillment.
Dwight Macdonald, quoting a friend in "Death of a Poet"

Those who knew James Agee best have often commented on—and
taken issue with—his absorbing, wide-ranging interests. When the
author's mentor and lifelong friend, Father James Harold Flye, first
met Agee, he was impressed by the breadth of the ten-year-old's curi-
osity. "He was . . . very intelligent and read quite a bit . . . We
talked a bit of the reading he'd done, a bit about pets and the woods
and fossils."[1] The schoolboy fancies became adult passions as Agee
developed discriminating opinions about photography and painting,
drama and music, and significantly, about film.

The spectrum of Agee's aesthetic fascinations is most revealingly
seen, however, in his literary endeavors; poetry, fiction, journalism,
screen-writing, and criticism were the touchstones of his career. Because Agee did not concentrate his literary efforts in a particular
genre, his life as a writer and as a man is the subject of considerable
discussion and debate.

Among those critics who believe that Agee's range of artistic endeavor prevented him from becoming a noted poet or novelist is
Dwight Macdonald. The man who secured the writer his first job as-

serts in *Against the American Grain* (1965) that his friend failed to write the work that might have made him a major talent. "Although he achieved much," Macdonald writes, "it was a wasted, and wasteful life."[2] Dwight Macdonald's judgment of the writer as a dilettante represents a school in Agee scholarship. The corpus of Agee criticism is divided roughly among three groups: a host of the writer's friends whose memoirs are colored largely by intimate association with him, biographers who speak of Agee both personally and professionally, and those scholars who address themselves primarily to his literary contributions.

Despite the variety of approaches taken in assessing James Agee, little scholarship has been done to support the proposition that the art imitated the life. Perhaps the critic who comes closest to suggesting a coherence in Agee's life and writing is Durant da Ponte. In a 1963 essay, "James Agee: The Quest for Identity," da Ponte suggests that the novelist used his fiction as a means of investigating his own past.[3] Actually, Agee's search for selfhood framed his life and lent order to the art that mirrored it. James Agee's life, like the lives of his personae, was grounded—however tortuously—in active, questing introspection. The enormous compulsion that Agee felt within himself to savor life in a Whitmanesque sense made his career appear chaotic. Yet behind literary projects begun and not finished, three marriages and two divorces, and endless bouts with tobacco, alcohol, and depression, there is a pattern: a need to bring the disparate elements into harmony, a rage to discover why, even as Rufus Follet wonders why, those whom he loved could "not now, not ever . . . not ever tell me who I am."[4]

The writing career testifies to the complexity of this author's makeup. As a man and as a writer, James Agee defied categorization or labels—a trait most conspicuously displayed in his fiction. It is precisely because of the disparate qualities that informed his personal and professional life that I will use an eclectic approach, virtually the only methodology available, to determine the extent to which James

INTRODUCTION

Agee used autobiographical writing as a means to sort out his own life. In seeking to explore the writer's quest for selfhood, a variety of resources have been used: primary materials, literary criticism, psychological studies on the effects of childhood bereavement, and interviews with members and friends of the Agee family. Agee's search for meaning focused on his need to find an approving earthly/heavenly father, his quest for a religious consciousness, and his self-destructive search for death.

1. James H. Flye, interview, December 28, 1976.
2. Dwight Macdonald, "Death of a Poet," *New Yorker* (November 16, 1957), 216.
3. Durant da Ponte, "James Agee: The Quest for Identity," *Tennessee Studies in Literature*, VIII (Winter, 1963), 25–37.
4. James Agee, *A Death in the Family* (New York: McDowell, Oblensky, 1957), 8.

TELL ME WHO I AM

CHAPTER
ONE

Early Life

All my people are larger bodies than mine, quiet, with
voices gentle and meaningless like the voices of sleeping
birds. One is an artist, he is living at home. One is a musi-
cian, she is living at home. One is my mother who is good
to me. One is my father who is good to me. By some
chance, here they are, all on this earth.
        James Agee, "Knoxville: 1915"

In the opening pages of *A Death in the Family*, James Agee pictures the
Knoxville that he knew as a child: the carved gingerbread on the Victorian houses, the softwood trees, the narrow yards, and the people
who lived there. It was the Agee and Tyler families who welcomed
young James Rufus Agee to "this earth" on November 27, 1909.

Agee's mother, Laura Whitman Tyler Agee, and father, Hugh
James "Jay" Agee, lived at 1505 Highland, two blocks from the
home of his Tyler grandparents. At the Tyler home lived two of the
persons referred to in "Knoxville: 1915," his mother's twin brother
Hugh, a talented painter and muralist, and his mother's younger sister Paula, a graduate of a music conservatory in New York City.
Agee's great aunt Jessie (who later left to found an Anglican con-
templative order at Chattanooga) also lived with Hugh and Paula
Tyler and their parents, Mr. and Mrs. Joel C. Tyler.

Laura Agee was descended from a "substantial family of artists and musicians," [1] which had come to Knoxville from Michigan near the close of the nineteenth century. Her mother was among the first graduates of the University of Michigan. Joel Tyler, Laura's father, was a prominent Knoxville businessman and a founder of the Ty-Sa-Man Machine Company. (Jay Agee worked for his father-in-law at Ty-Sa-Man.)

According to Laura Agee and Father Flye, "Joel Tyler was deeply attached to his grandson, whose intelligence and open-mindedness he admired," and Rufus, as Agee was called then, listened appreciatively to his grandfather. As he grew older, Agee delighted in his grandfather's blasphemy and agnosticism. In fact, "Agee liked to think he had adopted his grandfather's skepticism." Agee's grandmother was a genteel, aristocratic lady with artistic and musical gifts. "As a young child Rufus spent a great deal of time with his grandmother." He was extremely solicitous of Mrs. Tyler's forbidding deafness and eventual blindness. [2]

Jay Agee came from rural stock. His grandfather, James Harris Agee, had been a country doctor and politician of some renown in Campbell County, Tennessee. His father, Henry Clay Agee, had farmed and taught school in Campbell County until he died less than a month after his son Jay in 1916. His widow, Moss Lamar, lived until 1943. [3]

Although he had only finished the fourth grade, Jay Agee taught school briefly in LaFollette, Tennessee, where his family was then living. He subsequently took a position with the Post Office in Knoxville, and there Jay met Laura Tyler. After the young Agee's transfer to Cristobal, Panama, Laura asked her brother Hugh to make the voyage with her to the Canal Zone. The Tylers opposed the marriage,

1. Louise Davis, "He Tortured the Thing He Loved," Nashville *Tennessean*, February 15, 1959, p. 15.
2. Geneviève Moreau, *The Restless Journey of James Agee* (New York: copyright © William Morrow, 1977), 31–32. Miss Moreau obtained this information through interviews with Laura Agee Wright and Father Flye in 1964.
3. Charles W. Mayo, "James Agee: His Literary Life and Work" (Ph.D. dissertation, George Peabody College, 1969), 3.

but the wedding took place in 1906. The couple returned to the family farm near LaFollette two years later. After Jay's year with the Louisville and Nashville Railroad, near Corbin, Kentucky, the Agees moved to Knoxville in 1909.[4]

James Agee was deeply influenced by both of his parents. A Knoxville resident and lifelong family friend, Hazel Lee Goff, recalls the writer's father and mother: "He was a happy man, Jay; hearty and jovial and a wonderful husband and father. Laura, a more reserved and gently-bred person, responded wholeheartedly to his outgoing ways."[5] Young Rufus assimilated his father's generous and empathic spirit—qualities which Agee later emphasized in the character of Jay Follett in *A Death in the Family*. In the first chapter of the novel, Jay Follett takes his son Rufus into a bar and has a drink on his way home. Writes Agee of the little boy:

> He looked up his father's length and watched him bend backwards off in one jolt in a lordly manner, and a moment later heard him say to the man next him, "That's my boy"; and felt a warmth of love. Next moment he felt his father's hands under his armpits, and he was lifted, high, and seated on the bar, looking into a long row of huge bristling and bearded red faces. The eyes of the men nearest him were interested, and kind; some of them smiled. . . . Somewhat timidly, but feeling assured that his father was proud of him, he smiled back, and suddenly many of the men laughed. . . . His father smiled at him. "That's my boy," he said warmly.[6]

The open, joyously celebrative manner of Jay Agee was complemented by the retiring spirituality of his wife. Laura Agee, according to Hugh Tyler, possessed a "deep interest in church ritual."[7] Al-

4. Jeanne M. Concannon, "The Poetry and Fiction of James Agee: A Critical Analysis" (Ph.D. dissertation, University of Minnesota, 1968), 2.

5. Mayo, "James Agee," 16.

6. James Agee, *A Death in the Family* (New York: McDowell, Obolensky, 1957), 16, hereinafter cited in the text as *ADF* with page number.

7. Mayo, "James Agee," 21.

though the Tyler men were not church people and the Agee family only nominal Baptists, Agee's mother and grandmother were devout. Laura had a notion that southern gentilesse was inexorably linked with Christian devotion, and her strong Episcopal belief became an early shaping influence in her son's life—particularly following his father's death.

The car accident which took Jay Agee's life on May 18, 1916, made a searing impression on his young son. The swift violence of the event haunted him. Later, in *A Death in the Family* Agee chronicled the devastating impact of his father's death. The death created for six-year-old Rufus the anxious need to replace the loved, lost focus of his affection. Thomas Wolfe in *The Story of a Novel* expresses the young boy's quest.

> From the beginning . . . the idea, the central legend that I wished my book to express—had not changed. And this central idea was this: the deepest search in life, it seemed to me, that thing that in one way or another was central to all living was man's search to find a father, not merely the father of his flesh, not merely the lost father of his youth, but the image of a strength and wisdom external to his need and superior to his hunger, to which the belief and power of his own life could be united.[8]

The father is also the earthly representative of the Divine Being, and it is not surprising that Rufus Agee should reach out to a man who could embody that duality.

Agee's literal search for a father ended two years after his own father's death when, in the summer of 1918, Laura Agee took her two children to a cottage on the grounds of Saint Andrew's School, near Sewanee, Tennessee. Situated on the Cumberland Plateau, Saint Andrew's was founded in 1905 by a monastic order of the Episcopal church, the Order of the Holy Cross. There were various reasons for the Agees' summer stay in the mountains of middle Tennessee. Mrs. Agee had friends at Saint Andrew's, and since the area was two thou-

8. Thomas Wolfe, *The Story of a Novel* (New York: Scribner's, 1936), 39.

sand feet above sea level, the climate was much more pleasant than Knoxville. The most decisive factor in Mrs. Agee's desire to bring her family to "the mountain," however, seems to have been the religious atmosphere of the school. "Mrs. Agee had known of the place. . . . She knew of the Holy Cross fathers." [9]

Mrs. Agee returned to Saint Andrew's with Rufus and his sister Emma in the summer of 1919. It was during that time young Agee met the man who ultimately became his lifelong friend and mentor, Father James Harold Flye, an Episcopal priest and teacher of history. "And so began," Father Flye wrote, "one of the most cherished and rewarding relationships of my life." [10]

At the end of the summer, Laura Agee decided to move her family to Saint Andrew's permanently. A close friend of Mrs. Agee's, the editor of A Death in the Family, David McDowell, believes that the move was chiefly arranged "to be closer to the Order of the Holy Cross, to be closer to the rituals of the Church." In the fall of that year Rufus Agee enrolled as a student at Saint Andrew's. For most of the period between ages ten and fourteen, the boy Agee lived in the dormitory—"it being felt," Father Flye has written, "that this was better for him than living at home." [11] Laura Agee was particularly anxious that her son be in the company of men, in order that he might build a strong male self-concept.

The Saint Andrew's student body in 1919 consisted of about a hundred boys, a "very mixed, heterogeneous group," according to Father Flye. John Stroup, an early student at Saint Andrew's, remembered that the school was "rough, but good. Life was certainly not idyllic, and the student body was composed largely of poor mountain boys, fifteen to twenty per cent of whom were orphans, who wore torn overalls." Intellectually, the boys ranged from "deep country background, almost illiterate" to those who had good minds. Even among the latter group, Rufus Agee distinguished himself as one who "knew

9. James H. Flye, interview, December 28, 1976.
10. James H. Flye, "An Article of Faith," *Harvard Advocate*, CV (February, 1972), 15.
11. David McDowell, interview, December 30, 1976; Flye, "An Article of Faith," 17.

the answers to the questions that they asked him." So it was "in good humor" that Agee's classmates dubbed him "Socrates," [12] a name that later reappeared as Richard's nickname in *The Morning Watch*.

The school property was about two hundred acres—much of it in timber—with some land cultivated for farm use. There were a few houses, classrooms, and dormitories, and a small monastery. The spiritual tone of Saint Andrew's was set by the priests and monks who lived and worked there. When the school had been founded a dozen years earlier, the sight of the white cowls terrified the hill people, who called the clerics "Klansmen." An alumnus of the school, William Peyton, recalled that at Saint Andrew's in the early twenties, "the religious part of ones [*sic*] education was A MUST. . . . you had to have special permission, to be absent from any church service." [13]

Ten-year-old Rufus Agee was then an outgoing, inquisitive boy who delighted in reading and who eagerly sought to increase his knowledge. Father Flye was drawn to his young charge and wrote that from the outset "there were real bonds between us in spirit, feelings, and instincts." Flye found Agee "very tender-hearted, touched to quick sympathy and pity at the sight or thought of suffering, human or other, and incapable of willingly causing it. He had a keen sense of humor and comedy but was never comfortable with teasing or banter. He was by nature affectionate and trustful, with many endearing traits, and I felt deep tenderness and affection for him at this lovely age." [14] A Knoxville neighbor, Dr. A. B. Tripp, however, remembered Rufus as "strange and lonely. A boy who had never learned to play baseball." Mrs. Clyde Medford, who laughingly describes herself as "an old mountaineer," was a nurse at Saint Andrew's and neighbor to the Agee family. She remembers Rufus as "a good boy

12. Charles W. Mayo, interview with John Stroup, June 5, 1968; Flye, interview, December 28, 1976.
13. Flye, interview, December 28, 1976; *School on a Mountain*, documentary film of St. Andrew's School, St. Andrews, Tennessee, courtesy of the James Agee Memorial Library, St. Andrew's; William M. Peyton '25, to Walter B. Chambers, November 29, 1972, James Agee Memorial Library, St. Andrew's.
14. Flye, "An Article of Faith," 15.

6

. . . very active and very intelligent." He also seemed like a solitary child to her, with ways of his own: "The boys felt he was peculiar." Mrs. Medford believes that Father Flye responded empathically to the young Agee: "Father Flye took him under his wings. . . . He kind of looked after him, after Mrs. Agee came down here. . . . He stayed lots around Father Flye. . . . He treated him just like a father." [15]

Father and Mrs. Flye, who did not have any children, enjoyed a warm relationship with many Saint Andrew's students. Frequently, they would gather on the couple's front porch on Sunday afternoons for hot chocolate and cookies. Mrs. Flye would occasionally paint a portrait of one of the boys while the company played the piano and sang songs or simply chatted about the week's events.

Significantly, while a student at Saint Andrew's, Rufus Agee was free to visit the Flyes at any time, but was only allowed to see his mother once a week. Laura Agee sincerely wished to do the best for her son's welfare—entrusting him to sensitive and compassionate clergymen—but the injunction had a deeply wounding effect on the young boy. Agee's painful memory of watching his mother's cottage—clandestinely and brazenly—is feelingly recorded in *The Morning Watch*. As Geneviève Moreau concludes: "These solitary vigils must have been frequent, since Agee . . . used the 'watch' metaphor to refer to this period of his life." [16]

As a child, then, Agee was isolated by death and distance from his parents. Apart from the novella set at Saint Andrew's, the confused, betrayed attitude of the young Agee is also powerfully described in *A Death in the Family*. The writer's childhood sensations of loneliness and loss, which lingered on during his student days at the boarding school, find expression through the fictional creation of Rufus Follett's sister Catherine (a representation of Emma Agee and an older, more mature version of James Agee). On the morning the children

15. Dr. A. B. Tripp to Charles Mayo, April 13, 1968, in possession of Mr. Mayo; Mrs. Clyde Medford, interview, December 14, 1976.
16. Moreau, *The Restless Journey*, 47, 48.

were told that their father had died, Catherine wonders where he has gone:

> Her mother said he wasn't coming home ever any more. That was what she said, but why wasn't he home eating breakfast right this minute? Because he was not with them eating breakfast it wasn't fun and everything was so queer. Now maybe in just a minute he would walk right in and grin at her and say, "Good morning, merry sunshine," because her lip was sticking out, and even bend down and rub her cheek with his whiskers and then sit down and eat a big breakfast and then it would be all fun again and she would watch from the window when he went to work and just before he went out of sight he would turn around and she would wave but why wasn't he right here now where she wanted him to be, and why didn't he come home? Ever any more. He won't come again ever. But he will, though, because it's home. But why's he not here? (*ADF*, 257)

Catherine Follett's lack of comprehension and anger ring psychologically true. Such reactions, psychiatrists tell us, are a concomitant of death's impact on the child. In addressing himself to the question of childhood mourning, Dr. John Bowlby, a British psychiatrist and pioneer researcher in the field, notes, "Following unexpected loss there seems always to be a phase of protest during which the bereaved person is striving either in actuality or in thought and feeling to recover the lost object and is reproaching it for desertion." [17]

At the close of the "Knoxville: 1915" section of the novel, Rufus speaks of himself as being "familiar and well-beloved in that home" but adds, with stinging, poignant resentment, that those who love him "will not, oh, will not, not now, not ever; but will not ever tell me who I am" (*ADF*, 8). Rufus' keen pleading for his relatives to tell him why his father died and what his identity is as one bereft is full of suppressed hostility. That the event lingered unresolved in Agee's

---

17. John Bowlby, "Childhood Mourning and Its Implications for Psychiatry," *American Journal of Psychiatry*, CXVIII (December, 1961), 483.

mind is obvious in his commenting to his mother at age sixteen that he wanted to write about his father's death and its effect on those about him.[18] By that time the issue was ten years old. That Agee still felt the need to write about it testifies to the depth of his feeling for his father and to his perception of the death as an unresolved enigma.

The case of James Agee supports the clinical findings gathered by Bowlby and his associates. In a significant 1961 essay, "Childhood Mourning and its Implications for Psychiatry," Bowlby takes issue with the data of Melanie Klein who attributes pathogenic mourning to the loss of the breast (feeding and weaning) in the first year of life. On the contrary, Bowlby believes that the evidence suggests "that the most significant object that can be lost is not the breast but the mother herself (and sometimes the father), that the vulnerable period is not confined to the first years in childhood (as Freud . . . held), and that loss of a parent gives rise not only to primary separation anxiety and grief but to processes of mourning in which aggression, the function of which is to achieve reunion, plays a major part."[19]

On the topic of the effect of the loss of the mother versus the loss of the father, Bowlby in the same article concludes that, from birth to the age of five, the loss of the mother is the most telling. In discussing the period of latency and early adolescence, the psychiatrist addresses himself to Agee's situation, citing the studies conducted by Barry and Lindemann (1960) and Brown (1961), which show that the loss of the father between the ages of five and fourteen is "roughly equivalent to the loss of the mother."[20]

Given the weight of this psychological evidence and the description Agee gives of the mourning processes of the Follett children, who are mirrors of Agee's own grieved, confused notion of identity, it is reasonable to conclude that the death was for Agee a deeply perplexing, tragic mystery. In addition, Laura Agee was forced to as-

18. McDowell, interview, December 30, 1976.
19. Bowlby, "Childhood Mourning," 490.
20. Ibid., 494.

9

sume Jay Agee's authority in raising her son and Rufus no doubt chafed at the supplanting of his idolized father. Rufus' watching—in secret or in the open—contains a duality operative throughout Agee's life in relation to his mother. As a child and as an adult, he was frequently caught between the fear of encountering her displeasure and the wish to do so. Apart from the physical burdens that the living situation at Saint Andrew's imposed upon Agee, there were psychic burdens as well. His inability to become the head of the family was likely demeaning to his masculinity, and in a corresponding way, as an adult "Agee frequently experienced this same fear of failing the women he loved."[21]

In reaction to this repressive, vacuumlike situation within his immediate family, James Agee reached out toward the Flyes, and particularly toward the priest. Soon after his coming to Saint Andrew's, Rufus spent several afternoons a week taking French lessons from Father Flye "just for fun." The priest did not believe that his friendship with Agee was exclusive, but found in it "a special fullness of understanding and communication." The feeling was obviously mutual on Agee's part. "His relationship with Father Flye," David Dempsey writes, "became one of the unifying forces of his life."[22]

In the person of James Harold Flye, Agee had, as Mrs. Medford suggests, a father figure. Father Flye, perhaps out of modesty, does not see himself in that light. "Some have felt James Agee saw in me something of a surrogate for his father," Flye wrote in 1972, "but I do not think this was the case. Our friendship and association and feeling toward each other were such, it seems to me, as we might equally well have had if his father had been living."[23] But there is a good deal of evidence that Flye was indeed a surrogate father. David McDowell views Father Flye as at least a strong orienting figure in Agee's life.

21. Moreau, *The Restless Journey*, 47.
22. *James Agee: A Portrait*, Caedmon recording (TC 2042), Caedmon Records, New York; Flye, "An Article of Faith," 17; David Dempsey, "Praise of Him Was Posthumous," *Saturday Review*, August 11, 1962, p. 24.
23. Flye, "An Article of Faith," 16.

Dwight Macdonald, whose close friendship with Agee dated from Exeter days, shares my belief that Father Flye's genuine humility prevents him from making what he surely regards as a pretentious claim. Macdonald respectfully brushes aside the priest's objections, calling Flye "a real substitute father, in the Freudian sense."[24] Agee's own letters to the priest over three decades offer incontrovertible proof to hold against Flye's disclaimer.

It is in the collection of their correspondence, *The Letters of James Agee to Father Flye*, that the reader is reminded of the measure of Agee's devotion and love. A typical example (written from Phillips Exeter Academy in 1926): "Father, I do hope we'll see each other soon again. Occasionally I wake up with a jolt to the fact that I haven't seen you for over a year. . . . In getting these new friends and interests I don't forget you. But they pretty much absorb me, and I feel sorrier and sorrier that we can't be nearer together. I love you dearly, and I always shall."[25] Such a passage might be considered an example of youthful excess, yet the Agee-Flye correspondence is distinguished for its openness in the area of human feelings. The writer remained constant in his affection for the priest, as later letters indicate. In 1945 he wrote:

> Knowing each other many years, we don't often either say it or ever need to, yet occasionally, and now, it is a kind of luxury to say and realize how much I love you, how grateful I am to you, how greatly I value your friendship. . . . I never expect a relationship dearer to me, possible, than that I have nearly all my life had with you. I wish I could add to this honor I feel towards you, so clearly you could never doubt again, in any of the disappointments your life has known, how triumphant and great a life I feel yours is, and has always been. (*Letters*, November 27, 1945, pp. 154–55)

24. McDowell, interview, December 30, 1976; Dwight Macdonald, interview, December 30, 1976.

25. James Agee, *The Letters of James Agee to Father Flye* (New York: George Braziller, 1962) [December 14, 1926], 25, hereinafter cited in the text as *Letters* with date and page.

11

Five years later, Agee wrote from Los Angeles to thank Father Flye for a birthday letter. "It meant still more than usual to get it because I was alone out here, over my birthday, and I take birthdays hard. Mainly a kind of melancholy about my life, a sort of personal day of Atonement. And through the melancholy, a very deep sense of loneliness. So to hear from anyone I love, who loves me, is the best thing that can happen" (*Letters*, early December, 1950, p. 185). Beyond such sentiment, one is struck by the innocent, vaguely naïve tone with which Agee addresses the priest. In an astute observation, David Dempsey concludes that the letters "are pitched on the rather high plane of an adult who is anxious to maintain the good opinion of someone who has known him as a child." [26]

Dempsey's deduction raises a provocative question about the style and manner of the Agee-Flye correspondence. By virtue of his position as a clergyman, of course, Father Flye is an earthly representative of the Heavenly Father. While David McDowell states that for Agee, Flye was a "model priest," Dwight Macdonald extends the meaning: "Flye was certainly a spiritual father. . . . The tone of the letters attests to that." [27]

It is significant that both McDowell and Macdonald comment on the atypical nature of these letters. McDowell observes that the letters mention nothing about Jim's sexual habits (a common reference in letters to other friends) and have little to say about music, an area deeply important to him. Macdonald agrees. "The letters that I remember getting from him were much more secular. . . . He didn't express . . . his esoteric jeering in his letters to Flye." Likewise, Agee's correspondence with Walker Evans is revealing mostly for its sexual candor, bordering on crudity. [28] Beyond a question of differing tastes, it seems clear that Agee's epistolary relationship with the priest is not one between equals.

26. Dempsey, "Praise of Him Was Posthumous," 25.
27. Macdonald, interview, December 30, 1976.
28. *Ibid.*; the Humanities Research Center, the University of Texas at Austin, has in the James Agee Collection forty-six letters and cards from Agee to Walker Evans (1936–51).

The content of the letters, though, is more revealing than what Agee omitted. In commenting on Agee's customary practice of addressing him as "Dear Father," in his letters, Father Flye carefully points out that the term *Father* was "standard usage" at Saint Andrew's when speaking or referring to any priest. Nevertheless, several critics have pointed out the irony of the greeting. Indeed, as one *Time* reviewer observed, "Few sons have written to their natural fathers as James Agee wrote to Father Flye. Such trust, love and confidence in being understood seldom surmount the walls of consanguinity."[29]

James Agee, in short, was circumspect in his correspondence with the priest: anxious not to offend, yet equally desirous to confess the indiscretions that ultimately broke his health. Far from the flamboyant, faintly scandalous notes to his peers, Agee's letters to Father Flye are distinguished for their "confessional desire to relieve his own guilt" on a level that is serious, if not solemn, by comparison.[30]

Following Rufus' enrollment at Saint Andrew's, Father Flye naturally relieved Mrs. Agee of the bulk of her son's religious training and instruction. Mrs. Agee's decision to move her family onto the grounds of Saint Andrew's (though Rufus lived mainly in the dormitory), clearly announced the high priority that she placed on religious education. In recalling the years the Agee family spent at the school, Father Flye wrote of Laura Agee as a faithful churchwoman, possessing strong Anglo-Catholic convictions, and a genuine supporter of the spiritual emphasis at Saint Andrew's.[31]

Laura Agee was godmother to the first child of Mrs. Ann Tate, a Saint Andrew's neighbor. Mrs. Tate spoke of Agee's mother as "a religious lady . . . a wonderful Christian woman." Mrs. Agee, according to Mrs. Tate, possessed a lively sense of humor, but lived quietly and kept to herself. She was, apparently, devoted to taking care of the school chapel. Among other duties, she laundered the linens and kept the flowers fresh. Mrs. Medford recalls: "She took care of the chapel

29. Flye, "An Article of Faith," 16; "Unquiet One," *Time*, August 3, 1962, p. 60.
30. Macdonald, interview, December 30, 1976.
31. Flye, "An Article of Faith," 17.

as long as I knew her." Later, according to David McDowell, Laura Agee's deep piety caused some tension between herself and her son. Although she thought James a gifted writer, she "could not bear" the explicitly sexual passages of *Let Us Now Praise Famous Men*.[32]

The religious commitment of Saint Andrew's was at the core of the institution: "In the School, attendance was required at daily chapel service and on Sundays at the Sung Mass and at Evensong; Grace was said at meals in the School Dining Room; and religious instruction was a required course in the curriculum. There was due observance of Lent, Holy Week, and other special seasons and days of the Christian year, and Church boys were encouraged to go to Confession and Holy Communion." Rufus, not surprisingly, grew up with a solid foundation in this teaching and practice, and he was accustomed to the language of the Bible and the Book of Common Prayer. "He was an acolyte and used to serve often at the altar."[33]

Rufus Agee remained at Saint Andrew's School for four years and spent vacation visits at the home of his Tyler grandparents. When Joel Tyler's health declined in late February, 1924, Laura Agee moved to Knoxville with her children. Agee attended Knoxville High School in 1924–1925 before enrolling in Phillips Exeter Academy in the fall of 1925.

Even as her son had become immersed in the religious milieu of Saint Andrew's, so Laura Agee had found her own ties to theology and literature strengthened. In 1922 Agee's mother published a collection of twelve poems, *Songs of the Way*, a mix of religious and literary concerns. Two years later, Mrs. Agee married Father Erskine Wright, bursar at Saint Andrew's. The marriage was difficult for the adolescent Agee to accept, for he had never felt drawn to the priest. Agee found Father Wright "dry," with "no spark" to his personality. "Jim didn't like his stepfather," observes Agee's second wife. In his view, Father Wright was "narrow, moralistic, and rigid." Geneviève Mo-

32. Mrs. Ann Tate, interview, December 14, 1976; Medford, interview, December 14, 1976; McDowell, interview, December 30, 1976.
33. Flye, "An Article of Faith," 16–17; Flye, interview, December 28, 1976.

reau has written that, for the young man, "the marriage only seemed to justify anew the suspicion he had felt at Saint Andrew's: that his mother did not really care for him and would abandon him at the right opportunity." Following their marriage, the Wrights moved to South Carolina, then to Florida and Tennessee before settling permanently in 1926 at Rockland, Maine.[34]

Because of the friction between himself and his parents, it seemed natural for Agee to accept Father Flye's invitation to join him for a tour of France and England. The pair spent the summer of 1925 traveling chiefly by bicycle in the British Isles and on the Continent. It was a time when the bond between them was strengthened. In the following autumn Agee entered Phillips Exeter at Exeter, New Hampshire, as a sophomore and soon afterward, he dropped the name Rufus, which he disliked, and was thereafter known as Jim or James.

"Solitary by nature," Geneviève Moreau has written, Agee "became even more of a lone wolf at Exeter." The young man found the regimentation at the academy stifling and resolved not to become an "E man." His resultant nonconformity created several furors. The disciplinary council met to discuss his habitual tardiness at curfew, and all students were subsequently required to be in earlier, for example. Agee never intended to create a scandal, but his natural iconoclasm brought him into conflict with faculty and administrators. James Agee's off-campus meetings with Dorothy Carr, a worker at the Exeter Public Library, prompted schoolwide notice and general censure.[35]

Even though he frequently ridiculed what he felt to be hypocrisy and pretentiousness at Exeter, Agee participated in a wide range of school activities. The letters to Father Flye record his involvement in clubs centered around swimming, music, drama, and literature. Agee had a part in Exeter's production of *Katherine and Petruchio* and acted, as Baptista, in *The Taming of the Shrew*. When he entered the

34. Olivia S. Wood, interview, March 22, 1977; Alma Neuman, interview, March 21, 1977; Moreau, *The Restless Journey*, 56.
35. Moreau, *The Restless Journey*, 63.

academy, he began as associate editor of the *Phillips Exeter Monthly Magazine* and was later chosen editor-in-chief.[36]

Of all his course work and extracurricular activities, literature most absorbed the young Agee. His first Exeter letter written to Father Flye is significant in this respect: "My English work is most interesting of all. . . . I have blown myself and bought *Arrowsmith* and a few books. Have you read *Ariel*, a sort of fictionalized biography of Shelley? It's lovely. . . . I have just gotten Donn Byrne's *Blind Rafferty* from the very good library—but I haven't had time yet to read it" (*Letters*, October 19, 1925, pp. 17–18). Apart from telling the priest what he had read or intended to read, the letter is noteworthy because Agee expresses a keen ambition to write:

> I have written stuff for the *Monthly*, and I am to get a story and 2 or 3 poems in this month. This will get me into the Lantern Club, I hope. That is one of the big things to be in here. It runs the *Monthly*, and is a literary club. It gets several authors up each term who give very informal talks in the club room. Booth Tarkington, who graduated here, came several times, and Sinclair Lewis may come this winter. It's a swell idea to have such a thing in school, don't you think? (*Letters*, p. 18)

This interest in writing at Exeter was evidently something new. David McDowell asked Father Flye, "Did Agee show very early great interest and intelligence in, and about, creative writing?" Father Flye replied:

> I would say not at all, as far as I know, as long as he was at St. Andrew's. . . . I was not his English teacher, and I don't know what he may have done in papers for English, but I've known boys who were interested in writing when they were young. I've had a little boy come up to me at twelve years old and hand me a poem that he had written, and I would certainly encourage him. . . . sometimes

36. *Ibid.*, 64.

they would be very good poems. I never had anything like
that from Jim, not a word of poetry.

Instead, Father Flye traces Jim's literary awakening to their European
trip when he wrote descriptions of many places they visited.[37]

Agee's academic performance at Exeter was uneven, "alternately
mediocre and brilliant," and his teachers were often baffled by his
inconsistency.[38] He was passionately fond of English, history, and
Latin, but was a poor student in mathematics and the sciences. He
failed geometry and chemistry, for example, in his senior year. It was
in literature, of course, that Agee distinguished himself. He won the
Merrill Prize in English composition in 1927 and 1928, as well as the
Lantern Club English Prize, and became president of the Lantern
Club in 1927.

The letter of October 19, 1925, to Father Flye was a harbinger of
Agee's Exeter literary career and of his professional life. The prep
school years essentially marked the beginning of his writing interests, and he actively wrote, revised, and published numerous short
stories and poems during those student days. Jim, in the opinion of
Dwight Macdonald, "came alive" as a writer at Exeter. Macdonald,
who graduated from Exeter the year Agee arrived, says of the school
during his time there: "Exeter was the place for writers. It had a mar-
velous English Department." During the Exeter years, Jim Agee began thinking about serious literary projects. Shortly after his arrival
there, Agee said he wanted to write about the death of his father, although he was unsure of the form, whether poetry or prose. Says
McDowell: "He wasn't obsessed by this [his father's death], but this
was something that was in his mind all the time."[39]

---

37. James H. Flye, "Relationships with Agee" (panel discussion transcript, October
14, 1972, in James Agee Memorial Library, St. Andrew's School), 97. The panel included
Robert Fitzgerald, Father Flye, Andrew Lytle, Dwight Macdonald, and David McDowell.
38. Moreau, *The Restless Journey*, 64.
39. Dwight Macdonald, in the "Relationships with Agee" panel, p. 98; McDowell,
interview, December 30, 1976.

In a note written after the Christmas holidays in 1927, the neo-phyte author wrote rather romantically of recent self-discovery, "I've been reading *Leaves of Grass* since I came back. You know, since last winter or so, I've been feeling something—a sort of universal—oh, I don't know, feeling the beauty of everything, not excluding slop-jars and foetuses—and a feeling of love for everything" (*Letters*, December 31, 1927, p. 34). While the letter is rich in youthful sentiment, Agee's mother believed, as did Father Flye, that such an overflow of feeling was characteristic. "He loved life with a great joy and always with deepening reverence," Laura Agee Wright wrote in 1959, "so that every aspect of it was intensely important to him." [40]

Agee's interest in *Leaves of Grass* was part of his predilection for the romanticism of William Blake and A. E. Housman during this period. In 1929 during his freshman year at Harvard, Agee had already begun to scorn Whitman. He spoke derisively about his "W. Whitman stage about a year ago. . . . he seems generally half-assed to me now." But he still had a "rather conventional fondness" for Housman, a fondness he hoped to "never outlive," and he added that "it amounts at present more nearly to worship." [41]

The young writer's devotion to romanticism is also clearly seen in his writing during this period. Just prior to his graduation in May, 1928, the Exeter *Monthly* published Agee's most ambitious Exeter work, "Ann Garner." This hymn to nature celebrates the life cycle, drawing out themes of birth, fertility, sterility, and death, in narrative and dramatic form. Ann Garner, a mystical spirit who gives birth to a stillborn child, is also a life-giver and a plausible stand-in, in some sense, for Agee's own mother. The five-hundred-line poem explores themes that the young author would later detail in *The Morning Watch* and *A Death in the Family*.

The ideals of romantic literature also extended to Agee's private life. In Dorothy Carr, Agee found an intellectual soul-mate, a muse,

40. Mayo, "James Agee," 31.
41. James Agee to Dwight Macdonald, May 10 [1929], in possession of Macdonald, New York.

critic, and lover. The Exeter student read his poetry to the young woman for hours when she was seriously ill and bedfast for months. Agee even pledged to marry Dorothy Carr, but despite rumors of engagement when he left Exeter, the relationship ended quickly.[42]

In addition to his feeling for Dorothy Carr, Agee was also attracted to an Exeter boy and was crushed when the boy rejected his attentions. During this traumatic experience, Agee had read Dwight Macdonald's short story, "Wall," a tale of spurned love based on Macdonald's own Exeter experience. In his first letter to "Mr. Macdonald," then a Yale undergraduate publishing in campus literary magazines, Agee wrote candidly about the aborted affair:

> Last September I first read your story "Wall", —about the rise and decline of a friendship, if you don't happen to remember. It interested me then, and I liked it immensely. During this last term almost precisely the same thing happened to me—I being the Morris Cotesworth—the one who suffers. In my case there were consequences which you may possibly have thought of, but did not suggest—I was almost drowned in psychological meanderings, too dreary and far too long for any story. Quite frequently, I've been on the verge of suicide. Possibly mine was a more serious case, all the way through, though. At any rate "Wall" is now more to me than Gospel. I can read it over and recognize symptoms in every sentence. Were you yourself ever in such a fix? It seems impossible that you could have imagined so minutely such a story.[43]

In a subsequent letter to Macdonald, July 21, 1927, Agee commented further on the failed relationship with his fellow student: "His attraction should have been nil to me—and would have been, but for (1) adolescence and (2) the absence of girls 8 months of the year, as you said."

Agee was spending the summer vacation with his mother and

---

42. Moreau, *The Restless Journey*, 75.
43. James Agee to Dwight Macdonald, June 16 [probably 1927], in possession of Macdonald.

stepfather in Maine. He went on in the letter to tell his Yale friend that the weeks were passing with agonizing slowness: "I'd be grateful for a hoe and convenient corn; I'm finding life intolerably boring this summer. . . . there's nothing more diverting than an occasional movie and some glorious scenery."[44] It would appear that Agee had at best a limited relationship with his mother and Father Wright during this time. During these adolescent years, he made no mention of his parents in his letters to Dwight Macdonald and rarely wrote of them to Father Flye.

Despite the virtual noninvolvement with his immediate family, Agee wrote to Macdonald of his inability "to drive away my friends, so I get practically nothing done." Yet even with a circle of persons he could enjoy in Rockland, the young Agee was obviously lonely. He still expressed some anxiety about his sexual identity after the failed love affair with his classmate: "I'm unable, just now to imagine I'll ever feel any sexual emotion again. Of course I know I shall." As for young women in the Rockland area, Agee was in despair. In the late July note to Macdonald, he wrote of the void in his life with biting sarcasm, "I feel a great need for some girl or other, not for physical as much as for mental well-being. That's the hell of this lousy town; most of the girls are pleasantly moulded, but brains? (he laughs wildly). Really I wonder if I'll ever see a girl with whom I can discuss anything mutually more interesting than Ramon Navarro or So Big?"[45]

Even as his social life lacked a focus, the young writer was distressed by the forlorn state of his writing endeavors. In the same letter to Macdonald, Agee's literary and personal concerns are fused:

> Have you ever tried to write a play or story, and got into a hell of a muddle about what the next line or even word was to be? It's one of the most discouraging things on earth. Perhaps the most discouraging is to feel you've got a characterization just a little off, clear through. I'm trying

44. James Agee to Dwight Macdonald [July 21, 1927], in possession of Macdonald.
45. *Ibid.*

20

to write a novel now; I've just introduced a new man, and know I've got him entirely wrong, and that several hundred words are just one imaginative lie. . . .

During all last summer and so far now, I've written only about 20,000 words on the would-be novel. Worst of all, I feel my howl about lack of time is mainly bluff. . . . after a half-hour of desperate mental masturbation, all I produced was some lousy characterization.[46]

After Jim's graduation from Phillips Exeter in the spring of 1928, he entered Harvard University. The early Agee letters from Cambridge to Father Flye offer bright passing judgments on literature, music, and the people who surrounded him. A Harvard classmate, the poet Robert Fitzgerald, recorded his first impressions of Jim Agee, calling him "a rangy boy alert and gentle, but sardonic, with something of the frontiersman or hillman about him—a hard guy in more than the fashion of the time—wearing always a man's clothes, a dark suit and vest, old and uncared for, but clothes." In many respects, Agee's student years at Harvard were the fruition of the days at Saint Andrew's and Exeter. He made solid personal and professional alliances and entered into intellectual and artistic pursuits with a more sublime level of sophistication. E. Talbot Donaldson (Harvard, 1932), a classmate of Agee's, thought him unusually gifted, but especially recalls his decidedly unscholarly predilection for westerns. "He and I used to go occasionally to the movies together in Scolley Square in Boston. . . . Scolley Square was, of course, the throbbing part of the low section of Boston. There was an all-night movie there, where they wandered around with spray cans perfuming the atmosphere and also waking you up . . . if you went to sleep. And then we would walk home romantically into the dawn."[47]

Those who knew Agee at Harvard frequently have commented on his literary talent, readily apparent as an undergraduate. Donaldson

46. *Ibid.*

47. Robert Fitzgerald, "A Memoir," in *The Collected Short Prose of James Agee*, ed. Robert Fitzgerald (Boston: Houghton-Mifflin, 1962), 6; E. Talbot Donaldson, interview, November 12, 1976.

21

describes Agee as "Byronic": "He was terribly handsome with those blazing eyes . . . tall and thin and terribly intense. He did look," Donaldson concludes, "as if he had been nominated to be a poet." Of Agee in a course they shared—Robert Hillyer's class in versification—Robert Fitzgerald wrote: "We had been asked each to prepare a lyric for reading aloud. The figure in the front row on my right, looming and brooding and clutching his book, his voice very low, almost inaudible but deliberate and distinct, as though ground fine by great interior pressure. . . . So here, in the front row, were shyness and power and imagination." [48]

While Talbot Donaldson remembers the writer as being "elaborately witty" and one who "far out-distanced the Harvard boys," he acknowledges that he never felt entirely comfortable in his presence. Says Donaldson, "He was difficult. . . . There was an extraordinary level of unhappiness about him." [49] The notes to Father Flye underscore Agee's increasing penchant toward moodiness, and the letters quickly take on a portentous quality. "Rather often I get a horrible tight feeling as if I were wrapped in mummy-cloths. Sometimes I'm disgusted at myself, sometimes at the school or my friends—I was that way this evening—feeling inexorably like crying or biting into something or beating it with my fists" (*Letters*, March 17, 1927, pp. 27–28). Agee's curious feeling, as though he were bound up and unable to find constructive expression for the tremendous well of inner emotion, outlines a lifelong psychic dichotomy. Many people have spoken of Agee's generous compassion, but it is interesting to note that the depth of his feeling, as the excerpt cited suggests, could on occasion move him to violence. Robert Saudek, Agee's roommate at Harvard for four years, was struck by the paradox of a particular incident. During the second week of his freshman year, the autumn of 1928,

> Jim returned from his morning of classes looking like a volcano. He went over to the fireplace, turned and an-

48. Donaldson, interview, November 12, 1976; Fitzgerald, "A Memoir," 4.
49. Donaldson, interview, November 12, 1976.

nounced that he hated the place and hated a system that would seat "Agee" next to "Alsop" since that fat sonova-bitch, not yet having bought himself a Latin textbook, picked up Agee's new book, opened it up and broke its spine, then clearing a great hock out of his throat, spat it on the open page. Jim swung his fist against the stucco wall above the fireplace with all his might, abrading his knuckles, and he felt so ashamed of this display that he then struck the bleeding fist against his own temple and leaned spent against the wall. . . . That kind of eruption was awesome for Jim was the most compassionate person, and the least able to cope with insensitivity in others.

Talbot Donaldson, speaking of Agee's "very low boiling point," remembers a dinner for the staff of the *Harvard Advocate*. "We were entertaining . . . the head of the *Lampoon*. . . . Everybody was giving speeches. (In those days you put on a tuxedo and went to a hotel.) There was a small group. Agee was giving a speech and the *Lampoon* man kept making disagreeable remarks; and then Jim finally picked up his glass of whiskey and threw it in his face. . . . it was a characteristic time of loss of control.[50]

In an autobiographical piece Agee, speaking of himself in the third person, wrote half-jestingly of the tensions that informed his personality: "Due to some domestic or Christian trauma sustained in his early youth, he is kindly in proportion to his hatred."[51] The mock-heroic quality of the line does not obscure, however, the writer's ambivalence about his experience at Phillips Exeter. The later displays of rage and anger cited by Saudek and Donaldson could well have been a boiling over of the "horrible tight feeling," about which Agee complained in the letter from Exeter. The evidence suggests that the writer's displays of anger, though often fearsome in their magnitude, were relatively brief episodes and infrequent. These eruptions, family members and friends attest, were always accom-

50. Robert Saudek, "J. R. Agee, '32: A Snapshot Album, 1928–1932," *Harvard Advocate*, CV (February, 1972), 18; Donaldson, interview, November 12, 1976.
51. James Agee, "James Agee by Himself," *Esquire*, LX (December, 1963), 290.

panied by excessive self-recrimination and despondency—a lifelong pattern.

During his first summer at Harvard, Agee worked on a crew harvesting wheat in Nebraska and Kansas. The experience foretells, in microcosm, his bohemian existence in New York and prefigures, in some sense, his summer in Alabama in 1936. In the spring of 1929, he wrote Dwight Macdonald:

> I'm going to spend the summer working in the wheat fields. . . . The thing looks good in every way. I've never worked, and greatly prefer such a job; I like to get drunk and will; I like to sing and learn both dirty songs and hoboe ones—and will; I like to be on my own—the farther from home the better—and will; and I like the heterogenous gang that moves north on the job. You get a wonderful mess of bums and lumberjacks, so I'm told. Also I like bumming, and shall do as much of it as I can.[52]

The summer whetted Agee's sensual appetites. He was intoxicated by the experience of "bumming"—meeting new people, feeling fiercely independent. Like Thomas Wolfe's Eugene Gant striding across continents, Agee became something of a perpetual motion machine, maniacally questing, racing against time and a lack of money. Agee's letter to Macdonald of August 1 was "written in a wagonbed" because "about my only chance to write is between loads." "Have you ever done any bumming?" he asked. "It's funny business. In 24 hours I made over six hundred miles; in 23, I failed to make 28, was caught simultaneously by night and a cloudburst. I hope the good sort of luck prevails when I try to get home. I'm going to try to make it in 5 or 6 days, on ten dollars."[53]

When Agee returned to Harvard in the autumn of 1929, the carefree, loose style of living of the summer past, spilled over into his undergraduate career. More and more Jim began to take refuge in liquor: "Am drinking some; am not particularly fond of it," he wrote

52. Agee to Macdonald, Friday night, May 10 [1929], in possession of Macdonald.
53. Agee to Macdonald, ca. August 1 [1929], in possession of Macdonald.

to Father Flye in the autumn of 1929. "Gin, Rye, Scotch, etc. comprise the only commonly accessible drinks; and I prefer wine. . . . On the whole, an occasional bender satisfies me fairly well. Don't, please, get the idea that this invariably ends in drunkenness. That seldom happens unless I'm down in the dumps at the time" (*Letters*, September 29, 1929, pp. 44–45). Agee's penchant for alcohol, which became stronger with the passage of time, seemed to be inexorably linked to the same set of compulsions that led him into writing. In later years, liquor became a panacea for depression and a concomitant of writing.

Agee was consumed by the need to write and, not surprisingly, his Harvard letters reveal a deep interest in current books and literary figures: "Have you read Robert Frost's new book? I wish I could have a more unusual opinion of it, but . . . I think it falls a thousand feet below most of his other stuff. . . . Jeffers seems a good deal like Whitman at times—and, of course, a good deal more besides. . . . Have you read "A Farewell to Arms"? . . . He [Hemingway] seems tacitly to have admitted the repressed sentimentality of the other work . . . and the result is a great improvement." [54] Agee appeared to view his career as a writer with an alternate attraction and repulsion. The idea of being an author seemed to him a vocation forced upon him by fate about which he was deeply ambivalent. He wrote to Father Flye in 1930, "I'm from now on committed to writing with a horrible definiteness." Writing, in Agee's terms, was horrible because of the narrowness of its focus and its attendant cares. "In fact it amounts to a rather unhealthy obsession. I'm thinking about it every other minute, in one way or another; and my head is spinning and often—as now—dull with the continuous overwork" (*Letters*, November 19, 1930, p. 46).

By the beginning of his senior year, Agee was following a punishingly immoderate schedule that set the tone for future dissipation. Agee was named president of the *Harvard Advocate* in 1931, and by

54. Agee to Macdonald, April 24 [1929], [May 10, 1929], and [end of 1929], all in possession of Macdonald. Agee is probably referring to Frost's *West-Running Brook*, 1928.

25

Christmas he was physically and emotionally exhausted. "So I came back to Cambridge," he wrote to the priest in late December. "I was frantically reading for and taking exams which count 30% of four years work. Regularity began, and moderation ceased. . . . The regularity has been this: an average of 3½ hours sleep per night; 2 or 3 meals per day. Rest of the time: work or time spent with friends. About 3 nights a week I've talked all night" (*Letters*, December 27, 1931, p. 54).

Despite increasingly frequent drinking binges and academic probation, Agee managed to graduate in the spring of 1932 and was selected as the class poet. After delivering his ode (part of which he forgot) at Class Day, he attended commencement. By early afternoon he prepared to hitchhike to New York (to begin a job on *Fortune*). His roommate, Robert Saudek, recalls that last day after they had said "so long and good luck and write" and had shaken hands: "I remember looking down from the window as he emerged five stories below and hiked across the Eliot quadrangle with the heel-lifting stride he had brought with him four years before. . . . He still seemed like Rufus or Jim, and we wanted to cling to that, but soon thereafter and forever, the world would know him only as James Agee."[55]

55. Saudek, "J. R. Agee," 21.

CHAPTER
TWO

Starting Out

One gusty day . . . as we were crossing 49th street, Jim
and I halted in the Radio City wind and sunlight to agree
with solemnity on a point of mutual and long-standing
wonderment, not to say consternation: how rarely people
seem to believe that a serious writer means it; he means
what he says or what he discloses.
                    Robert Fitzgerald, "A Memoir"

It was during his presidency of the *Advocate* that James Agee, together with Talbot Donaldson, wrote a wildly popular parody of
Time. On the strength of this issue and the intervention of Dwight
Macdonald, Agee was hired as a cub reporter on *Fortune* in the
Chrysler Building. (Later he was given a staff position at the magazine.) Despite this promising start, the neophyte writer slipped into a
serious depression in August of that first New York summer. He
wrote openly and revealingly to Father Flye: "Father, I can't tell you
what I mean about this or anything else. I've been used to bad spells
of despondency always, but this is something else again; it seems to
be a rapid settling into despair of everything I want and everything
about myself. If I am, as I seem to be, dying on my feet mentally and
spiritually, and can do nothing about it, I'd prefer not to know I was
dying." This vision of the end of life lead him to confess further: "I've
felt like suicide for weeks now—and not just fooling with the idea,

but feeling seriously on the edge of it. . . . I know I should be able to fight my way out of this, and I hate and fear suicide, but I don't have a thought that isn't pain and despair of one sort or another. Knowing how rotten the thoughts are, instead of making them better makes the whole thing worse." The self-loathing that led to these suicidal thoughts pervades the letter. "I simply am not capable," he wrote, "of being the kind of person, doing the kinds of things, which I want to be. And I haven't enough good in me to realize the filthiness of this discontent, and to reconcile myself to it. I would certainly prefer death to reconciling myself." The letter closes with an apology and a plea for understanding: "One of the damnable things about me now is that when I write or speak to anyone I love, I become so fouled in my own rottenness that I can write nothing else. . . . God bless you and help me." [1]

This letter of 1932 provides an unusually frank description of Agee's precarious mental state. It is clear that he recognizes this depression as being significantly different from the other "bad spells of despondency." Agee is, in fact, exhibiting the classic symptoms of what Freud called melancholia. According to Freud, the patient who suffered from melancholia would experience "a lowering of self-regarding feelings to a degree that finds utterance in self-reproaches and self-revilings, and culminates in a delusional expectation of punishment." [2] Agee's references to "the filthiness of this discontent" and the "damnable" problem of becoming "so fouled in [his] own rottenness" clearly exemplify the "self-reproaches and self-revilings" of which Freud writes. In addition, and perhaps most important, there is also an expectation of punishment: "I seem to be . . . dying on my feet mentally and spiritually and can do nothing about it." The tone and theme of self-deprecation in this letter is sounded repeatedly in

1. James Agee, *The Letters of James Agee to Father Flye* (New York: George Braziller, 1962), August 14, 1932, pp. 56–57, hereinafter cited in the text as *Letters* with date and page number.
2. Sigmund Freud, "Mourning and Melancholia," in James Strachey (trans. and ed.), *The Standard Edition of the Complete Psychological Works of Sigmund Freud* (23 vols.; London: Hogarth Press, 1957), XIV, 243.

the Agee-Flye correspondence. In a 1962 review of the *Letters*, again paralleling Freud's definition of melancholia, John Updike was moved to write: "The truth is that we would not think of Agee as a failure if he did not insist on it himself. . . . These letters brim with self-accusations." [3]

The letter is also significant for the murky psychology at work in Agee's mind. The writer's youthful confessions jibe well with Walker Evans' description of his friend's "paralyzing, self-lacerating anger." [4] The note to Flye indicates Agee's willingness to commit violent self-destruction ("not just fooling around with the idea"), and it recalls his earlier statement about being "kindly in proportion to his hatred." The writer's explanation for that description—that he suffered "some domestic or Christian trauma" in early childhood—although glibly made, raises a question about the relationship between Jay Agee's death and his son's depressions.

In "Mourning and Melancholia" Freud emphasized the importance of the "loved object" in depression, but he did not directly link childhood bereavement and adult depression. Subsequent research in the area of childhood bereavement, however, suggests that in many individuals a direct correlation can be found. In an essay on childhood mourning Dr. Felix Brown, a psychotherapist and leading authority on grief in children, states that he "frequently" finds that parental death is a "highly significant" event in his patients' lives, "appearing to determine their subsequent neurotic and depressive reactions." Likewise, the data of Dr. John Bowlby strongly corroborates the conclusion that a substantial number of persons with depressive symptoms, "especially those who are actively suicidal," have experienced parental loss during the early years. [5]

3. John Updike, "No Use Talking," *New Republic*, August 13, 1962, p. 23.
4. Walker Evans, "James Agee in 1936" (Foreword), in James Agee, *Let Us Now Praise Famous Men* (Boston: Houghton-Mifflin, 1960), ix.
5. Freud, "Mourning and Melancholia," 243; Felix Brown, "Childhood Bereavement and Subsequent Psychiatric Disorder," *British Journal of Psychiatry*, CXII (October, 1966), 1036; John Bowlby, "Childhood Mourning and Its Implications for Psychiatry," *American Journal of Psychiatry*, CXVIII (December, 1961), 495.

These findings do not imply that mental illness or chronic depression follows in all cases of parental death. Some children display pathological grief, but others express healthy grief. How a child copes with his bereavement seems to depend generally upon how the resulting circumstances of the death are handled. In the case of James Agee it appears that his father's death set up a depressive syndrome within him. He could not let go of its meaning for him. The death of Agee's father may also have made him a compulsive worker. Felix Brown believes that a normal child can withstand the trauma of a parental death if capable resources are provided. Whether or not suitable follow-up assistance is provided, though, Brown maintains that parental death "can, in some circumstances, prove even to be an incentive to great achievement, as in the many poets, writers . . . who have been orphaned."[6]

We cannot determine whether Agee felt the need to justify his existence and thereby to assuage his childhood guilt at living when his father had died. Certainly he had a rage to be successful. The etiology of the depressions appears to have been a mystery to Agee himself. Short of trying to explain conclusively the nature of the writer's mental processes, what can be said is that he felt despondent about his inability to realize the goals that he set for himself. Agee's sense of irony and paradox was powerful and continually emphasized for him the pain of his own life. In a 1930 letter to Father Flye, he captured the tensions in his existence: "Life is too short to try to go further into details about this. But it's part of what serves to keep me busy; and unhappy. The whole thing still seems just within the bounds of possible achievement; but highly improbable. There are too many other things crowding in to ruin it: the whole course of everyday life" ([November 19, 1930], *Letters*, 49). Four years later, he expressed the same problem more succinctly: "how to become what I wish I could when I can't."

Agee's uncertain self-image seems to have been a force at work in

6. Brown, "Childhood Bereavement," 1040.

his attraction toward Olivia "Via" Saunders, whom he had met at Harvard and with whom he later fell in love. Some months before their marriage in January, 1933, Agee wrote of the dynamics of their relationship and about himself: "I have a hideous trait of moodiness and worse which from time to time does bad things to both of us; but I'm trying as never before to understand, control it, or at worst control my reactions to it, and thank God, am making some headway. It's the sort of intangible, slippery thing that I guess is worst in the world for two fairly nervous people to cope with; and when it's out of hand, neither of us has an easy time" ([October 25, 1932], *Letters*, 63). The letter returns to Agee's earlier fated notion about his depressions. "I'm sometimes really forced to believe I have a dirty and unconquerable vein of melancholia in me; but I know this hypochondrical [*sic*] feeling is the most dangerous imaginable to it" (*Letters*, 63). The letter then moves guiltily away from this point toward naming himself as the cause. "I know the most important faculty to develop is one for hard, continuous varied work and living; but the difference between knowing this and doing anything consistent about it is often abysmal. Along with the melancholia, or part of it, is rotten inertia and apathy and disgust with myself" (*Letters*, 63).

The "rotten inertia" that Agee was feeling had a traumatizing effect on him. He was mentally and, in some sense, physically frozen into passivity during this period. In another letter written in the fall of 1932, dated "Oct. the hell," to "Brother Ethelbert" Donaldson, Agee speaks of "a gruesome sense of not being fit for society: just one of the Misfits, if you get what I mean, who moped in the fiftieth story of this chromium tower being dominated by the Machine and feeling more & more like hell and a heel. All this means that I often wanted to call you up and get drunk or even just Talk and watch life go by, and twice even had one trembling hand on the receiver." [7]

It is plausible that Agee, because of his considerable self-denial and ambivalence, felt yoked to writing as a vocation. In a field in

7. James Agee to E. Talbot Donaldson [1932], in possession of Donaldson.

31

which one is only as competent as his last work, writing set up for him unreal professional expectations to match his own personal desires. Agee was forever on a maniacal quest for selfhood, forever discontented and dissatisfied. The chronic pitfalls of "rotten inertia and apathy and disgust" never permitted Agee to have a realistic view of himself. The negative aspects of his personality tempered his success enough so that he was always preoccupied with his own failure, but the furies, though they ultimately drove him inward upon himself, were not powerful enough to force him to give up writing.

Throughout his life and his long, bruising search for himself, Agee was tied to the secure, affirmative center of his life, Saint Andrew's. It was to Father Flye that Agee turned for counsel and guidance inasmuch as the priest seemed to him to embody the godly virtues of patience, wisdom, love, and perhaps most important, understanding. Having found in Father Flye an earthly/heavenly father figure, Agee moved out into the world's arena to work out the relationship between religion and life. Agee's religious consciousness, which was first awakened by the piety of his mother, was later transferred to Saint Andrew's by virtue of his student involvement there and his friendship with the priest.

It is reasonable to assume, however, that Agee remained devoted to his father's memory in part because he saw him as one who lived out Christian ideals of charity, compassion, and generosity. The writer's own life, then, because of the significance of both parents' lives, became a bridge between the doctrinaire ways of his mother and the celebrative manner of his father. In attending Saint Andrew's and in developing his intimate association with Father Flye, Agee honored his mother's wishes; but in his refusal to become a practicing Christian, and in his unwillingness to accept certain doctrinal statements, Agee remained true to Jay Agee's spirit.

While attempting to merge and synthesize his parents' conflicting beliefs, Jim Agee made his own theological position clear, according to Father Flye: "As between the essentially religious and the non- or anti-religious, there is no doubt whatever in which category

James Agee belongs. Read "Dedication" in his book of poems."[8] "Dedication," the middle poem of his premier book of verse, *Permit Me Voyage*, represented "a first systematic effort to straighten out," in the words of W. M. Frohock, "the conflicts, and particularly the conflicting loyalties of his own life." For Frohock, *Permit Me Voyage* "revealed a kind of agonized self-searcher," who wished to identify and pay homage to the influences of his life and then move on.[9]

Permit Me Voyage, and particularly "Dedication," serves as a kind of autobiographical summary of Agee's life up to that time. Beyond those who personally affected his existence, Agee dedicated the volume "in much humility to God in the highest."[10] He began in Whitmanesque fashion by dedicating the work "to those who in all times have sought truth and who have told it in their art or in their living; Christ, Dante: Mozart: Shakespeare: Bach . . . the fathers of Holy Scripture: Shelley: Brahms: Rembrandt . . . Lawrence: Van Gogh: and to an unknown sculptor of China, for his god's head" (*PMV*, 16). Apart from those cited in the opening stanza who helped to remake civilization, Agee focuses on the multitude who lived lives of pain or who died in obscurity: "Those of all times who have sought truth and who failed to tell it in their art or in their lives. . . . those who died in the high and humble knowledge of God: seers of visions; watchmen, defenders, vessels of his work; martyrs and priests and monarchs and young children and those of hurt mind; and to all saints unsainted" (*PMV*, 16).[11]

The poem assumes a religious world view, as the writer offers benediction and absolution to those who died like his father "in glory of peace, nor hope nor thought of any glory: to those who died in sorrow,

8. James H. Flye, "An Article of Faith," *Harvard Advocate*, CV (February, 1972), 22.

9. W. M. Frohock, "James Agee: The Question of Unkept Promise," *Southwest Review*, XLII (Summer, 1957), 221.

10. James Agee, *Permit Me Voyage* (New Haven: Yale University Press, 1934), 10, hereinafter cited in the text as *PMV* with page number.

11. The poet's reference to "saints unsainted" is doubtless witness to Agee's romantic belief in the holy qualities of the unrecognized mass of humanity, not a pejorative comment aimed at the orthodox church for dereliction of duty.

and in kindness, and in bravery; to those who died in violence suddenly" (*PMV*, 16). Agee addresses the mass of humanity in the poem,
speaking of those who died prematurely or without opportunity to
complete their lives: "those who died virgin: or barren . . . those who
took their own lives into the earth; . . . those who died in deadly sin"
(*PMV*, 16).

The poem progresses from the general to the specific, and Agee
seems to recall his mountaineer forebears when he speaks of those
whose lives were "frustrate with circumstance . . . who never knew
truth, nor much beauty, and small joy but goodness of endurance; to
all those who in all times have labored in the earth and who have
wrought their time blindly, patient in the sun" (*PMV*, 16). In suc-
ceeding paragraphs the poem names certain family members who
died, among them "James Agee my brave father." To them and to all
those who died in whatever condition, the poet ends with the blessing "May they rest" (*PMV*, 17).

The subsequent stanzas of the eight-page poem stand as a hymn
to the living, to those who are conscious of their mortality: "Via, my
wife . . . my mother . . . my sister Emma . . . James Harold Flye,
priest, who befriended my boyhood with the wisdom of gentleness,
and to Grace his wife . . . a dozen friends, who know their names"
(*PMV*, 17). This second section offers tribute to a variety of figures as
disparate as Ring Lardner, Abraham Lincoln, Charles Spencer Chaplin, Ivor Armstrong Richards, Pablo Picasso, Walker Evans, and
Scott Fitzgerald. To his distinguished collection of artists, critics,
and statesmen, the youthful poet offers an apologia "for my dulness
and . . . shame for my megreness [*sic*] and caution" (*PMV*, 17).

The next verses of "Dedication" catalog unnamed persons of every rank and station, and the condition in which they live: "farmers
and workers and wandering men and builders and clerks and legisla-
tors and priests and doctors and scientists and governors of nations
and engineers and prisoners and servants and sailors and merchants
and soldiers and airmen and artists; in cities amassed, and on wide

34

water, and lonesome in the air, and dark under the earth, and laboring in the land, and in the materials, and in the flesh, and in the mind, and in the heart" (*PMV* 22). In his final series of dedications, Agee couches the images in a theological context. In his naming of "the Holy Catholic and Apostolic Church," he dedicates the poem to the world created by the Alpha and Omega: "To the entire hierarchy of the natural God, of every creature lone creator, in his truth unthinkable, undimensionable, endlessness of endlessness: beseeching him that he shall preserve this people" (*PMV*, 22).

Agee concludes the poem with an invocation of the Kyrie Eleison: "O God, hear us. O God, spare us, O God, Have mercy upon us" (*PMV*, 23). The poem moves generally into a liturgical confessional, but one laced with doubt as to the existence of the creator: "Not one among us has seen you, nor shall in our living time, and may never. We fumble all blind on [*sic*] the blind dark, even who would know you and who believe your name" (*PMV*, 23). His mother's piety and his father's agnosticism are equally evident. Although the poet wants to embrace dogma, given the nebulousness of the Godhead, he questions the beliefs: "Little as we know beyond the sill of death do we know your nature: and the best of our knowledge is but a faith, the shade and shape of a dream, and all pretense" (*PMV*, 23).

A variation of the Kyrie is repeated in the last stanza: "Have mercy upon us therefore, O deep God of the void" (*PMV*, 23). In the final line, Agee closes with a prayer for purity of vision: "And make the eyes of our hearts, and the voice of our hearts in speech, honest and lovely within the fences of our nature, and a little clear" (*PMV*, 23). It was this informing religious consciousness that became James Agee's credo and quest, as he endeavored to learn from humankind the meaning of divine lessons: "A way to hear, and a way to see, and wisdom, and careful love" (*PMV*, 23).

As in his mother's poems, *Songs of the Way*, the verse of *Permit Me Voyage* is significant for Agee's blending of religious and literary themes. The merging of these elements was at the heart of "Dedica-

35

tion": "It is a dedication of all I am or can be: to God, to truth, and to Art which is both." [12]

The reviews of the book—and particularly of "Dedication"— were generally unfavorable. Lincoln Kirstein wrote that the prayer-poem was "a hymn of praise, compassion, and a curse of genuine proportions." His was one of the few perceptive comments. Reviewers as a whole were at a loss to explain Agee's method. "It embarrassed them to find a prayer in the midst of a book of poetry." [13]

Robert Fitzgerald, however, saw the book as "the work of a desperate Christian," and "Dedication" as a series of "strenuous prayers." He summarized the critical reception of the work as blind to its uniqueness. "So far as I can discover, none of the contemporary comments on it, including the Foreword by MacLeish, took much notice of what principally distinguished it at the time: the religious terms and passion of several pieces." [14] The clearly supplicatory tone of the work, the poet's beseeching of blessing and benediction, and the humility of the presentation, made "Dedication" a significant religious and literary testament of Agee's early personal and professional life. The middle poem is the portrait of the young artist, fumbling "all blind on the blind dark." Although the book had literary merit and Agee benefitted as a writer from doing such a catalog, *Permit Me Voyage* was a financial disaster. Less than six hundred copies were sold the first year.

In November, 1935, Agee took a leave of absence from *Fortune* to spend time writing in a remote section of Florida, Anna Maria Key. During this time, November–May, 1936, Agee totally involved himself in learning the craft of writing. The writer's desire to internalize the method of his art is strongly echoed in a February letter to

12. Jeanne M. Concannon, "The Poetry and Fiction of James Agee: A Critical Analysis," (Ph.D. dissertation, University of Minnesota, 1968), 64.

13. *Ibid.*; Frohock, "The Question of Unkept Promise," 221.

14. Robert Fitzgerald, "A Memoir," in *The Collected Short Prose of James Agee*, ed. Robert Fitzgerald (Boston: Houghton-Mifflin, 1962), 23.

Father Flye: "I just know that I have a terrible amount to learn, un-learn, reclaim and discipline in myself" ([February 17, 1936], *Letters*, 84).

The writer who appealed to Agee most during this period was James Joyce. Robert Fitzgerald remembered a copy of *Ulysses* in Agee's bathroom: "Joyce engrossed him and got into his blood so thoroughly that in 1935 he felt obliged, as he told a friend of mine, to master and get over that influence if he were ever to do anything on his own." Along with this passion to "master" Joyce during the winter at Anna Maria, Agee also had a developing interest in psychology. "He was now steadily devouring Freud and recording his dreams," Fitzgerald writes of Agee's notes during that year. " 'Read Freud until midnight' is an entry several times repeated. There are pages like Stephen's or Bloom's waking thoughts in Ulysses." [15]

Agee's fascination with James Joyce is not surprising. The anti-orthodox stand of the two writers is remarkably similar. Eugene Webb explored the subtleties of Joyce's climactic scene in *A Portrait of the Artist as a Young Man*: "—Heavenly God: cried Stephen's soul, in an outburst of profane joy." According to Webb, *profane* for Joyce does not mean the opposite of *sacred*, but rather communicates "that sense of the numinous described by Rudolf Otto, the sense of a mystery both awesome and fascinating, charged with intrinsic value." Stephen's decision to pursue a secular vocation, like Richard's in *The Morning Watch*, grows in part from a desire to move beyond the constricting authority and narrow interpretation of the institutional Church. It is the world of "profane joy"—the melding of the sacred and secular—that moved both authors and their creations. One suspects that Agee would have understood perfectly Stephen's reference to God as a "shout in the street." Eugene Webb's point is well taken. The breadth and complexity of Joyce's religious comprehension and measure of belief mitigates against theological reductionism in his

15. *Ibid.*, 29.

37

case. As with Agee, "Joyce's mind was 'super-saturated' with religion in which he disbelieved, and his idea of the opposing forces that made up human life was given a special character by his persisting Catholic sensibility." [16]

It was at Anna Maria, significantly, that Agee wrote the auto-biographical, Joycean prose of "Knoxville: 1915." In a "half-filled" notebook, the writer outlined the possibility for the work: "Have been working (c. 12–15,000 words) on the footloose in Knoxville idea. Don't know." [17] In the spring of that year, after completing narrative and other sections of A Death in the Family, the writer and his wife, Olivia, drove to Saint Andrew's. Once established at the Flye's cottage, Agee read "Knoxville: 1915" to the priest.

After a month's stay with Father and Mrs. Flye, the Agees returned to New York. Of this pilgrimage back to his boyhood school (Agee's first since 1924), more will be said in the third chapter. But that the mountain—and the company—still claimed his deepest affections is obvious: "I agree with Mrs. Flye: no time or visit ever, anywhere, has been so good and meant so much to me. Much love to you both. Rufus" ([June 18, 1936], Letters, 92).

In the same letter, Agee outlined his next Fortune job, an assignment that would eventually grow into Let Us Now Praise Famous Men: "Have been assigned to do a story on: a sharecropper family (daily & yearly life) . . . Best break I ever had on Fortune. Feel terrific personal responsibility toward story; considerable doubts of my ability to bring it off" (Letters, 92). As the task was conceived by Fortune, Agee together with the photographer, Walker Evans, "on loan from the Farm Securities Administration," would spend a portion of the summer months living with three Alabama tenant families. Agee's initial excitement, though tempered by grievous self-doubts, did not wane. From the beginning, he committed his heart's blood to the project. Of their eight weeks on the assignment, Walker Evans wrote, "Agee

16. Eugene Webb, The Dark Dove (Seattle: University of Washington Press, 1975), 114, 118.
17. Fitzgerald, "A Memoir," 31.

worked in what looked like a rush and a rage. In Alabama he was possessed with the business, jamming it all into days and the nights. He must not have slept. He was driven to see all he could of the families' day, starting, of course, at dawn."[18]

The time spent in southeastern Alabama was for Agee a rare opportunity that "opened the way for a new round of self-examination." It became a kind of testing ground for him, a place to measure the depth and sincerity of his middle-class morality and ethical system. The *Fortune* assignment provided a natural way to experiment with the "conflicting loyalties" that were so much a part of "Dedication." Despite the fact that the book was to be about sharecroppers in the South, the subject, as a variety of critics have noted, is Agee himself. "His real, deep subject was not the sharecroppers themselves," states W. M. Frohock, "it was the emotional experience of meeting the fact of the sharecroppers." Victor Kramer agrees: "*Let Us Now Praise Famous Men* . . . is as much about Agee the reporter as it is about the farmers with whom he lived." In a 1961 essay, Erling Larsen summarizes this argument, drawing a Whitman-like parallel, "We should remember that the hero of Agee's book is really himself."[19]

The young writer journeyed to a place in Alabama, eighty miles from Birmingham, which he called Cookstown. Agee altered the names of the three interrelated families he lived among, as well, calling them the Rickettses, the Woodses, and the Gudgers. For just under a month, Agee and Walker Evans stayed with George and Annie Mae (Woods) Gudger and their four children, ranging in age from ten to twenty months. Of the three families, Agee found the Gudgers "the most nearly representative" (*LUNPFM*, 414).

It is clear from near the beginning of the book how much James

18. James Agee, *Let Us Now Praise Famous Men* (Boston: Houghton-Mifflin, 1960), xiii, hereinafter cited in the text as *LUNPFM* with page number; Walker Evans, "James Agee in 1936," Foreword in Agee, *Let Us Now Praise Famous Men*, xi.
19. Frohock, "The Question of Unkept Promise," 221, 225; Victor A. Kramer, "Agee's Use of Regional Material in *A Death in the Family*," *Appalachian Journal*, I (Autumn, 1972), 72; Erling Larsen, "Let Us Not Now Praise Ourselves," *Carleton Miscellany*, II (Winter, 1961), 94.

Agee wanted to be accepted by these families and the people he lived among. In 1936 "Agee," according to Walker Evans, "was a youthful-looking twenty-seven. I think he felt he was elaborately masked, but what you saw right away—alas for conspiracy—was a faint rubbing of Harvard and Exeter, a hint of family gentility, and a trace of romantic idealism" (*LUNPFM*, ix). The writer's desire to remain "elaborately masked" remained uppermost in his mind, lest he give an impression of superiority. Walker Evans was struck by the young man's need for approval. "He won almost everybody in those families—perhaps too much—even though some of the individuals were hard-bitten, sore, and shrewd" (*LUNPFM*, xi). The Alabama experience obviously appealed to Agee's sensibilities, to his "great capacity for understanding and compassion."[20]

Agee was touched by the childlike affection that the tenants had for him: "In some bewilderment, they yet love me, and I, how dearly, them; and trust me, despite hurt and mystery, deep beyond making of such a word as trust" (*LUNPFM*, 189). Agee felt a rare communion with the sharecroppers. He wrote feelingly of the lamplit evenings spent with George and Annie Mae after the children had been put to bed. "We held quietness, gentleness, and care toward one another like three mild lanterns held each at the met heads of strangers in darkness" (*LUNPFM*, 414).

Those persons who knew James Agee well have frequently commented on the depth of his caring. "Jim's most important quality," for David McDowell, "was his *empathy*, his total absorption with another person." Agee's generosity with friends in trouble is legend. McDowell recalls that in New York he "ran a private psychiatric clinic all his own." This "overflow of sympathy," as his mother described it, made it impossible for Agee to separate himself from the problems of his friends or even strangers. Agee's compassion, according to Dwight Macdonald, so lacked boundaries that it was tantamount to masochism. "He listened, and not only listened . . . no

20. Flye, "An Article of Faith," 22.

matter who he was talking to, and how idiotic their ideas were, he never put them down, he never dissented; in fact, he always found something to agree with. . . . He endured bores and cranks and nuts. . . . Agee seemed to be unable to reject any invasion of himself or idea.[21]

Let Us Now Praise Famous Men is replete with illustrations of the writer's empathy. At the beginning of book two he tells of a trio of young black men "only twenty to thirty, yet very old and sedate," who had been "sent for by a running child":

> They had been summoned to sing for Walker and for me, to show us what nigger music is like (though we had done all we felt we were able to spare them and ourselves this summons). And they stood patiently in a stiff frieze in the oak shade, their hats and their shirts shedding light, and were wanting to be noticed and released, for they had been on their way to church when the child caught them. . . . Meanwhile, and during all this singing, I had been sick in the knowledge that they felt they were here at our demand, mine and Walker's, and I could communicate nothing otherwise; and now, in a perversion of self-torture, I played my part through. I gave their leader fifty cents, trying at the same time, through my eyes, to communicate much more, and said I was sorry we had held them up and that I hoped they would not be late. (*LUNPFM*, 28–29, 31)

The concern of the young writer that the Alabamans not be exploited, embarrassed, or humiliated is expressed variously throughout the narrative. A leaf from Agee's forty-page *Famous Men* notebook is suggestive of how he regarded the three musicians and their situation. The page contains only one entry: "Certain normal predicaments of human divinity."[22]

21. McDowell, quoted in Charles W. Mayo, "James Agee: His Literary Life and Work," (Ph.D. dissertation, George Peabody College, 1969), 131; *Ibid.*, 162; Macdonald, interview, December 30, 1976.

22. James Agee, "Let Us Now Praise Famous Men" (notebook in Humanities Research Center, University of Texas at Austin).

Agee's shame and sense of poignancy with the black trio prefigures an oft-quoted incident described a few pages later in "Near a
Church." As James Agee and Walker Evans were out riding one day,
they went around a curve and saw a country church. The church was
locked and Evans wanted to photograph the rude, austere interior
furnishings. While the two men were wondering whether to crawl
through a window, a young black man and woman went by on the
road. With their grave looks, the couple made them feel "ashamed
and insecure" in their desire "to break in and possess their church"
(LUNPFM, 40). After several moments, the writer decided to go
after them, to ask their permission or to see if they could direct him to
a minister. "Before I had gone ten steps they turned their heads (toward each other) and looked at me briefly and impersonally, like
horses in a field, and faced front again; and this, I am almost certain,
not through having heard sound of me, but through a subtler sense"
(LUNPFM, 40–41). When Agee's foot twisted in the gravel, however, "the young woman's whole body was jerked down tight as a fist
. . . the rear foot skidding in the loose stone so that she nearly fell,
like a kicked cow scrambling out of a creek, eyes crazy, chin stretched
tight, she sprang forward into the first motions of a running not
human but that of a suddenly terrified wild animal. In this same instant the young man froze, the emblems of sense in his wild face wide
open toward me, his right hand stiff toward the girl" (LUNPFM, 41).
The couple came to a stop, the man talking to the woman and
protectively placing his hand on her shoulder. "I came up to them,"
says Agee,

> and stopped a yard short of where they, closely, not touch-
> ing now, stood, and said, still shaking my head (No; no; oh,
> Jesus, no, no, no!) and looking into their eyes; at the man,
> who was not knowing what to do, and at the girl, whose
> eyes were lined with tears, and who was trying so hard
> to subdue the shaking in her breath, and whose heart I
> could feel, though not hear, blasting as if it were my whole
> body, and I trying in some fool way to keep it somehow

relatively light, because I could not bear that they should receive from me any added reflection of the shattering of their grace and dignity, and of the nakedness and depth and meaning of their fear, and of my horror and pity and self-hatred; and so, smiling, and so distressed that I wanted that they should be restored, and should know I was their friend, and that I might melt from existence: "I'm *very sorry*! I'm *very* sorry if I scared you! I didn't mean to scare you at all. I wouldn't have done any such thing for anything. (*LUNPFM*, 41–42)

There was then an awkward moment, with neither the couple nor Agee saying anything. In this instant, the writer wanted physically to demonstrate that he meant no harm, that he cared for them.

The least I could have done was to throw myself flat on my face and embrace and kiss their feet. That impulse took hold of me so powerfully, from my whole body, that I caught myself from doing it exactly and as scarcely as you snatch yourself from jumping from a sheer height: here, with the realization that it would have frightened them still worse (to say nothing of me) and would have been still less explicable; so that I stood and looked into their eyes and loved them, and wished to God I was dead. (*LUNPFM*, 42)

Apart from scaring the couple, Agee was pained that he had to explain why he stopped them because in that area blacks never dismissed a white man or appeared to be bored with his conversation (*LUNPFM*, 42). The man and woman, he writes, did not know the answer to his question, a response "usually safest for negroes to say." After thanking them and apologizing once again, the writer "nodded, and turned away from them, and walked down the road without looking back" (*LUNPFM*, 43).

Jim Agee's overwhelming desire to prostrate himself "and embrace and kiss their feet" is an emblem of his compassion and is a metaphor for the work as a whole. *Famous Men* powerfully intimates—and the variant pages for the work confirm—that the writer was not only touched by the massive deprivation around him, but also admired the sharecroppers for their "simple and terrible work." The book has frequently been criticized for lack of objectivity. Agee is faulted for overidentifying with the people he lived among. Alan Holder, for example, observed that "Agee, reacting against a general feeling of condescension toward tenants, tried to canonize them."[23]

The fact that Agee's series of articles grew to a lengthy book is itself testimony to the depth of his commitment and his belief. It is in the variant manuscript for the work, however, that Agee becomes maudlin and sentimental. He devotes long passages in the excised sections to minutely cataloging the labors of tenant men, women, and children. He writes of work from which there "never will be any escape except briefly in extreme sickness and finally in death." In the variant text, by way of sensitizing the reader to the "stupefying" monotony of a tenant woman's work, he suggests cooking the same breakfast, lunch, and supper each day for thirty days, using no meat except fried or broiled salt pork. The writer also recommends washing the same few dishes three times a day for a month, thinking of it as a practice multiplied by twelve months a year for a lifetime.[24]

"Of the man's work," Agee writes, "I know of no way you can get an idea short of taking his place." Nevertheless, he offers a few ideas which, if acted upon, help to approximate the lot of the male tenant farmer:

> For one month: or you might use for it your next vacation: do either the hardest manual work you can find or contrive, or do setting-up exercises and liftings of weights. Do these, if possible, in the broad heat of the hottest sun available. Whether it is work or exercise you are doing, begin it at about six in the morning, and do not stop for more than an aggregate of ten minutes in the middle of the day. Dur-

23. Alan Holder, "Encounter in Alabama: Agee and the Tenant Farmer," *Virginia Quarterly Review*, XXXII (Spring, 1966), 199.

24. James Agee, "Let Us Now Praise Famous Men" (typed and typed carbon copy manuscripts, incomplete, in Humanities Research Center, University of Texas at Austin), n.p.

ing all this time, do not borrow, have no conversation with anyone who is not an unskilled laborer or a member of his family; do no reading, nor writing, nor hearing nor playing of music or news, nor looking at paintings, use only tactile words and ten of the plainest generalizations you can think of, and wherever you go, go on foot unless you can obtain a mule.[25]

The variant manuscript describes in exacting detail the labors of children, who, from the time they are able to stand, feel the obligation and necessity of picking cotton. Children, says Agee, are born into sharecropper families to work. As they grow older and learn to drag the cotton bag, which holds up to a hundred pounds, hour after hour in the searing heat, the picking for them "quickly absorbs more and more . . . the flat and finally demolished taste of drudgery."[26]

These passages make clear the extent of James Agee's sympathies. He was in awe that the labor was not only excruciating, but also unending. The tenant families he observed engaged in tasks each of which "is the weight of not merely of itself, but of itself in the twenty thousandth repetitions [sic], with twenty thousand more to come." And these repetitions, he writes in the variant text, form themselves into weeks and seasons of "blue carbons of one another, the letters less and less legible."[27]

The reality of this toil was perhaps too painful for the young man's romantic idealism to bear, for Agee came to see a kind of nobility in the sharecroppers' mean poverty and labor. "So deeply did he admire these people," Erling Larsen has written, "and, indeed, love them that it became in his mind a sin to pity them." Compassion, the critic believes, was defined by the writer in its primary sense: "He wanted and needed to suffer with these people."[28] Not surprisingly, then, the tenant life cycle became for him a "heroic

---

25. *Ibid.*, n.p.
26. *Ibid.*, n.p.
27. *Ibid.*, n.p.
28. Larsen, "Let Us Not Now Praise Ourselves," 93.

dance," which "unfolded, slow, gradual, tremendously and quietly weighted" (*LUNPFM*, 323).

So it was that Agee came to believe, with a curious mixture of envy and dread, that the tenants' severe deprivation allowed them— in the simplest, most elemental way—to be closer to the life force and, therefore, to God. As the "Near a Church" segment forcefully suggests and as Walker Evans maintained, Agee thought of the share-croppers as divine creations: "After a while, in a round-about way, you discovered that, to him, human beings were at least possibly immortal and literally sacred souls" (*LUNPFM*, xii). In the last pages of the book, Agee records an image of the Gudger's youngest child, Squinchy, nursing. For the writer, the baby became a representation of God-in-man: "I see how against her body he is so many things in one, the child in the melodies of the womb, the Madonna's son, human divinity sunken from the cross at rest against his mother" (*LUNPFM*, 442).

It was, of course, James Agee's experience of living with and among the three families that caused him to feel a mystical bond between them—and sharecroppers generally—and himself. In the preface to the book, Agee states that it is not possible to adequately represent tenantry in the United States by focusing on one family; but adds that by observing three families, it was felt it might be done with "qualified adequacy" (*LUNPFM*, xiii). This prefatory statement is a cautious reworking of a variant text included in the *Famous Men* notebook: "We are satisfied that they adequately represent white cotton tenants." In a two-page "explanation" from the notebook, Agee expands on the meaning for him of the assignment and of the families. The passage is significant for the unmistakable quality of religiousness that he believes is at the center of the tenant experience of the sharecroppers: "They represent; they are; not only tenantry, not only tenants. . . . They are also sons and creatures of God; and they are God; and in essence this volume begins, with what inadequacy will be naked before you, an enquiry into human divinity."[29]

29. Agee, "Let Us Now Praise Famous Men: Notebook," 14.

46

From the beginning of the "enquiry," the writer had pledged to immerse himself in the milieu of the sharecroppers, to experience their culture on their terms. In recalling their arrival among the families, Agee speaks directly to the figures in the book, remembering Fred Ricketts' "droughted corn," Paralee Ricketts' cornshuck hat, Louise Gudger's "clean dress" and the "quiet glowing gold color" of her skin (*LUNPFM*, 362–63, 366–67). The tone of "First Meetings" is warm and intimate, as the writer reflects about Evans and himself being driven out to the Ricketts' home, where George Gudger and Bud Woods joined the company. Agee remembers Evans taking pictures on a side of the porch, with the group sitting around and talking, "eating the small sweet peaches that had been heating on a piece of tin in the sun, and drinking the warm and fever-tasting water from the cistern sunk beneath the porch" (*LUNPFM*, 362).

Beyond such willingness to observe amenities and the generous character of the writer's spirit, "First Meetings" is significant for the repetition of Agee's guilt feelings: "And we kept you from your dinners an hour at least; and I was very sorry and ashamed of that then, and am the same at all times since to think of it" (*LUNPFM*, 362). This is the same sort of guilt that Agee experienced with the trio of musicians and the couple in "Near a Church." Guilt was a constant in Agee's life. Mia Agee, the writer's third wife, has written that Agee's was "a sense of guilt that at times could paralyze him and that at the same time formed a very basic part of his character." [30]

Let Us Now Praise Famous Men displays Agee's keenly felt anxieties and fears. Numerous passages of the book also reveal Agee's sexuality and his interest in sexual imagery. In describing the Ricketts' world, Agee writes of the house and the sleeping family within, where "naked side by side those brothers and sisters, those most beautiful children; and the crazy, clownish, foxy father; and the mother; and two old daughters; crammed on their stinking beds, are resting the night" (*LUNPFM*, 76). The writer's awareness of an excruciating

---

30. Mia Agee with Gerald Locklin, "Faint Lines in a Drawing of Jim," in David Madden (ed.), *Remembering James Agee* (Baton Rouge: Louisiana State University Press, 1974), 160.

47

lack of privacy, of entire families sleeping in one room, leads him to meditate in a later section on the growth of tenant families. Agee employs theological language to inform his image of creation: "Here we have two, each crucified, further crucify one another upon a shallow pleasure of an iron bed and instigate in a woman's belly a crucifixion of cell and whiplashed sperm" (*LUNPFM*, 76).

This brief passage rightly suggests a broad range of sexual expression in *Famous Men*, ranging from subdued lust ("shallow pleasure of an iron bed") to a religious vision of God divinely fulfilling his purpose through earthly creatures ("crucifixion of cell and whiplashed sperm"). Two notions of sexuality—as erotic and as filial love—are combined in the figure of Emma Woods's first marriage. Agee describes her as a fertile, bovine creature, "a big child, sexually beyond propriety to its years" (*LUNPFM*, 62). Evans and himself, Agee explains, are sexually attractive to her, and "each of us," he writes, "is fond of her, and attracted toward her." The writer says that before she must leave to join her husband, "Emma could spend her last few days . . . having a gigantic good time in bed . . . with Walker and with me" (*LUNPFM*, 62).

The writer's fantasy did not become reality, but when this sexually ripe girl must take her leave, she moves the writer to deeper feeling with her sublime goodbye: "I want you and Mr. Walker to know how much we all like you. . . . We wisht you wasn't ever going away but stay on here with us, and I just want to tell you how much we all keer about you" (*LUNPFM*, 64). Touched, Agee writes, "What's the use trying to say what I felt." This somewhat wanton child, who appeals to him in an erotic sense, has claimed his filial love as well: "I had such tenderness and such gratitude toward her that while she spoke I very strongly . . . wanted . . . to take her large body in my arms and smooth the damp hair from her forehead and to kiss and comfort and shelter her like a child" (*LUNPFM*, 65).

Cognizant of the physical and mystical qualities of the sharecroppers' fleshly bodies, the writer was also sensitive to the material extension of them—their clothing. He was entranced by overalls and found in the denim hues an aesthetic and ethereal beauty. Agee was also intrigued by the consummate effect of age, sun, washing, sweat, and use on the overalls—how they evolved "into realms of fine softness and marvel of draping and velvet plays of light" (*LUNPFM*, 267). In the section "Three women's dresses," the writer describes the garments of Mrs. Gudger, Mrs. Woods and Mrs. Ricketts. He notes with painful accuracy the harsh folds, the crude stitching of the fertilizer sacks cut into work dresses, the dark grease and sweat on the coarse material. Agee describes with equal precision the overalls of the men. They represent, for him, an indigenous bit of Americana, a symbol of an impoverished class. Overalls to the southern working man, he writes, "are his uniform, the badge and proclamation of his peasantry" (*LUNPFM*, 265). Because of the abject severity of the garments, they achieve a kind of rare purity, a terrible sort of elegance: "One could watch and touch even one such garment, study it, with the eyes, the fingers and the subtlest lips, almost illimitably long, and never fully learn it; and I saw no two which did not hold some world of exquisiteness of its own" (*LUNPFM*, 267).

Indeed, in Agee's view, the denim and fertilizer sacks of the tenant man and woman became virtually religious garments. He describes them in terms that might be used in talking of the hair shirts of medieval ascetics. These are garments worn only by those initiated into the mysteries of a cruelly simple life. In his chronicle of the rooms of the Gudger house, Agee expands upon this notion of clothing as prized, holy objects of adornment. One day after Annie Mae and the children had left for the morning, he opened drawers and looked under beds. Later when Agee heard the family approaching, he felt as if he had committed a sacrilege, had violated the pristine quality of their poverty, and had destroyed their faith in him: "I hear her voice and the voices of her children, and in knowledge of those hidden places I have opened, those griefs, beauties, those garments whom I took out, held to my lips, took odor of, and folded and re-

49

stored so orderly, so reverently as cerements, or priest the blessed cloths, I receive a strong shock at my heart, and I move silently, and quickly" (*LUNPFM*, 188).

The houses of the tenant families, as shelters for these holy innocents and repositories for their "exquisite" belongings, are, from Agee's perspective, veritable temples. The writer uses biblical imagery to describe these structures, in which "the bone pine hung on its nails like an abandoned Christ" (*LUNPFM*, 19). In the Gudger's house he calls one decorated wall, containing the fireplace, mantle, and hearth, "the altar"; the table in front of the fireplace, which holds a mixture of prosaic and precious items, is "the tabernacle" (*LUNPFM*, 162, 165). At the end of day, he writes, "the whole home is lifted before the approach of darkness as a boat and as a sacrament" (*LUNPFM*, 220).

Agee was as impressed by the stark simplicity of the tenant houses as he was by the severe, harshly tailored clothes of the sharecroppers. The houses were winsomely unpretentious creations that gave aesthetic pleasure: "It is my belief that such houses as these approximate, or at times by chance achieve, an extraordinary 'beauty'" (*LUNPFM*, 202). The Gudger's house became an ideal of poverty—a rude manger that appeared "most earnestly handmade, as a child's drawing, a thing created out of need, love, patience, and strained skill in the innocence of a race" (*LUNPFM*, 143).

At the end of *Famous Men*, Agee weaves the imagery of sexuality, clothing, and the house to talk about himself. In the section "In the Room: In Bed," he graphically describes the difficulty he experiences one evening in sleeping. Stripped and lying in bed, he notes that the bedding is cold and "almost slimily or stickily soft," the mattress lumpy, the springs weak, the pillowcase smelling like "old moist stacks of newspaper" (*LUNPFM*, 424–25).

Attempting to distract himself, Agee fantasizes about the purpose of the bed: "I tried to imagine intercourse in this bed; I managed to imagine it fairly well" (*LUNPFM*, 425). Bedbug bites bring his reverie to an abrupt end. He strikes a match and kills a batch of them, finding fleas in the process. The presence of the fleas unnerves the writer, and strongly aware of the "bare wood," his "bare feet," and his "stark nakedness," he gets up and goes out to the porch. Walking out into the yard, the young man feels the wet clay earth and engages in a brief communion with the night: "The instant I was out under the sky, I felt stronger than before, lawless and lustful to be naked, and at the same time weak. . . . I looked straight up into the sky, found myself nodding at whatever it was I saw" (*LUNPFM*, 426).

When Agee returns to his bedroom, he dresses and goes to bed fully clothed, but the vermin attack the exposed portions of his flesh. He strips once again, shakes out his clothes, dresses a second time, and climbs into bed. He can still feel the bedbugs "nibbling" under his clothes. He smokes, looks up at the holes in the roof, and thinks about the experience outside: "I don't exactly know why anyone should be "happy" under those circumstances, but . . . I was: outside the vermin, my senses were taking in nothing but a deep-night, un-meditatable consciousness of a world which was newly touched and beautiful to me, and I must admit that even in the vermin there was a certain amount of pleasure" (*LUNPFM*, 427–28).

In his essay on *Famous Men*, Erling Larsen speculates that Agee wanted to expose himself physically to the vermin because "he in his work was physically exposing others."[31] It is a plausible explanation for the psychology at work in Agee's mind, but the passage is note-worthy for its merging of physical sexuality and consciousness of the created universe. In imagining intercourse in the bed, Agee casts himself as a metaphorical partner who is only able to consummate his fantasy by communing with the night, with God. He experiences bliss after this mystical union; he is "happy." The bedbugs serve to remind him of God's creation; and as he feels them biting his flesh, he admits "there was a certain amount of pleasure." More significantly, during the experience Agee becomes unified with the sharecroppers and embraces their lot. Through the epiphany, the writer becomes a

31. Larsen, "Let Us Not Now Praise Ourselves," 94.

twentieth-century Saint Francis, ascetically giving thanks for small joys in the midst of deprivation. Agee's nocturnal experience, then, is symbolic of a physical and spiritual seeking after enlightenment.

Because James Agee was touched by the sublime quality of the poverty he encountered, he was genuinely ambivalent and baffled about the medium to convey the experience: "If I could do it, I'd do no writing at all here. It would be photographs; the rest would be fragments of cloth, bits of cotton, lumps of earth, records of speech, pieces of wood and iron, phials of odors, plates of food and of excrement" (*LUNPFM*, 13). Dwight Macdonald believes that Agee will be remembered for *Famous Men* and principally for the "peculiarly hopeless form" that Agee selected.[32]

While the work does, in one sense, defy categorization, many critics have spoken of its theological dimensions. By design, it contains a variety of religious elements: the use of biblical language and the rubrics of church ritual, the naming of Jesus Christ as an "unpaid agitator" in the description of the book's characters, the title from Ecclesiasticus, the extensive scriptural references, and the section on the Gudger's family Bible, are examples. But it is the content that bespeaks Agee's religious vision. As Erik Wensberg notes, "The smoke clearly indicates the source of the fire." Wensberg, among others, points out that "the prose . . . is most often written in the cadences of the Bible and the organ and the Protestant hymnal."[33]

For Dwight Macdonald, Agee's desire to work with an iconoclastic form to make, as he says, his "big statement," was symptomatic of the writer's "strong masochistic tendency." Despite his sense of the book's importance Agee seemed to downplay it when he cautioned the reader in the preface, "Above all else: don't think of it as Art" (*LUNPFM*, 15). His ambivalence about the book, manifested in his earnest wish that his work not be worshiped and the anxious, exhaustive negotiations with *Fortune*, Harper, and Houghton-Mifflin to

32. Dwight Macdonald, interview, December 30, 1976.
33. Erik Wensberg, "Celebration, Adoration, and Wonder," *Nation*, November 26, 1960, p. 418.

get it published, was an outgrowth of his personality. Dwight Macdonald describes it in this way: "He certainly didn't take any guff from any editor or anyone else, but by the same token, he was passive and masochistic about his fate." [34] The opposing forces of Agee's intense need for success and his despair of achieving it are apparent in an incident at the publisher's office: "At Houghton Mifflin in Boston they still remember a meeting that Paul Brooks, an editor there, had with Agee and Evans to talk over the format in which they were going to publish *Let Us Now Praise Famous Men*. When they came to the kind of paper it should be printed on, Agee said he thought the best thing would be newsprint. Brooks took this in and said mildly, 'But, Jim, newsprint! In fifty years newsprint will crumble away to dust.' And Agee said, 'That's what I mean.'" [35]

Agee had been troubled from the onset of the project about the commercial aspects of publishing the book. "It seems to me curious, not to say obscene and thoroughly terrifying," he wrote in his preface,

> that it could occur to an association of human beings drawn together through need and chance and profit into a company, an organ of journalism, to pry intimately into the lives of an undefended and appallingly damaged group of human beings, an ignorant and helpless rural family, for the purpose of parading the nakedness, disadvantage and humiliation of these lives before another group of human beings, in the name of science, of "honest journalism," of humanity, of social fearlessness, for money. (*LUNPFM*, 7)

The four years between James Agee's graduation from Harvard and the summer of 1936 had been varied and difficult. During that time he had had his first job, his first serious depression, and his first marriage. The publication of *Permit Me Voyage* in 1934 had brought with it a new direction. In commenting on a line in the final poem of

34. Macdonald, interview, December 30, 1976.
35. Robert Fitzgerald, "Agee Library Dedication Banquet Transcript," (October 14, 1972, in James Agee Memorial Library, St. Andrew's School), 114.

53

that volume ("My heart and mind discharted lie"), Robert Fitzgerald writes of these early post-Harvard years, "His purpose was to rechart, to re-orient himself, by reference to the compass needle itself, his own independent power of perception, his own soul." [36] James Agee's drive to "re-orient himself" through the religious consciousness that he sought was the outcropping of an odyssey that began inchoately after his father's death, later took on form and shape at Saint Andrew's, and finally crystallized while he lived among the tenant families. The writer's "enquiry into certain normal predicaments of human divinity" was not to end with *Famous Men*, the religious vision that he forged during the Alabama assignment fused with his physical and emotional self. The mark of that summer, and his bond with those women and men with whom he lived, never left him.

36. Fitzgerald, "A Memoir," 24.

CHAPTER THREE

Uncharted Paths

In the circles he frequented, everyone was pretty intense.
They smoked, drank, talked, sat up late, wandered around
the Village looking for company, dreamed of greatness,
fought off sterility, just as he did. But it was more or less
understood that Agee was special. There was a unique energy in him just as there was a unique beauty in his voice,
eyes and hands.

F. W. Dupee, *King of the Cats and Other Remarks
on Writers and Writing*

As James Agee became an accepted member of the New York literati,
he affected the life-style embraced by numerous artists living there in
the 1930s. Yet even in that bohemian atmosphere, the young writer
distinguished himself. "His intensity was different from that of others that we knew," F. W. Dupee wrote. "He smoked and drank as if to
appease an elemental hunger rather than to satisfy a nervous craving."
In Agee's own "mordant vita" written for *Esquire* in 1942, he described himself as "shy at parties, though not antisocial in the clinical
sense." His own favorite places for chatting *tête-à-tête* were "quiet corners behind layettes or refrigerators."[1]

1. F. W. Dupee, *King of the Cats and Other Remarks on Writers and Writing* (New York:
Farrar, Straus, and Giroux, 1965), 80; James Agee, "James Agee by Himself," *Esquire*, LX
(December, 1963), 290.

Once stationed in an agreeable spot, Agee would speak passionately, nodding with emphasis "while he sliced, carved and scooped words out of the air with his hands." In many of the all-night sessions, the writer drank "as unawarely as breathing in great easy draughts." Among his contemporaries, Agee was regarded as a "heroic drinker" with a great capacity for liquor. Yet Robert Fitzgerald maintains, as do others of the writer's circle, that he never saw the writer inebriated.[2]

The early New York years set a pattern of dissipation that was to characterize the writer's adult life. Mia Agee has stated that her husband was simply temperamentally unable to take care of himself. Dwight Macdonald agrees: "Even for a modern writer, he was extraordinarily self-destructive." The collective weight of his after-hours conversations, his penchant for alcohol, tobacco, and women, gave him, in Dwight Macdonald's words, "the worst set of habits in Greenwich Village."[3]

The not surprising concomitants of the writer's steady drinking were his periodic, severe depressions. There is substantial evidence to link Agee's chronic melancholia with his father's death, but it is also a fact that alcohol functions as a depressant. One may easily visualize the writer's cyclic problem of seeking relief through drink from "the most possible kinds of pain, mental and spiritual," as he wrote to Father Flye in the fall of 1934, only to feel ultimately more despondent. In the same letter to the priest, Agee pointed to his central problem: "How to become what I wish I could when I can't." The writer's inability to assuage his intense desire for approval and his inability to grant himself mental well-being drove him further into despair. Agee's October, 1934, letter mentioned the possibility of sui-

2. Dupee, *King of the Cats*, 80; Louis Kronenberger, *No Whippings, No Gold Watches* (Boston: Little, Brown, 1970), 139; Robert Fitzgerald, "A Memoir," in *The Collected Short Prose of James Agee*, ed. Robert Fitzgerald (Boston: Houghton-Mifflin, 1962), 42.
3. Dwight Macdonald, interview, December 30, 1976; Mia Agee with Gerald Locklin, "Faint Lines in a Drawing of Jim," in David Madden (ed.), *Remembering James Agee* (Baton Rouge: Louisiana State University Press, 1974), 160; Dwight Macdonald, "Death of a Poet," *New Yorker*, (November 16, 1957), 216.

cide, for he wrote, the depression was "fierce and complicated enough to keep me balancing over suicide as you might lean out over the edge of a high building, as far as you could and keep from falling but with no special desire not to fall." [4]

During this period Agee was moved, on at least one occasion, to act out his self-destructive impulses. One day during that October, the writer's coworker at *Fortune*, Wilder Hobson, went into Agee's office on the fiftieth floor of the Chrysler Building. Hobson "saw only his hands clinging to the outside window sill" and was terrified to witness the writer "hovering over the Manhattan void." Agee's friend, traumatized by the scene, waited behind the door until the writer climbed back into the cubicle. Hobson then "found Agee to be strangely calm and he took care not to reveal his own fright." [5]

Agee was always regarded as something of an oddity at *Fortune*. Co-workers frequently found him working in the middle of the night. Editors and staff members were hard-pressed to know how best to use his talents. Consequently, the writer was given a host of exotic assignments—an in-depth study of Brooklyn, an article on orchid growing, another on railroads, and so on. Agee's final drafts, although usually written in beautifully executed prose, frequently did not fit the style of the magazine. The piece about the borough of Brooklyn, written with considerable understanding and precision, was nevertheless considered "too strong" for print. The article subsequently had to be rewritten by someone else. [6]

Even as the writer was dogged by writing problems during this period, he was beset by marital difficulties as well. James Agee's marriage to Olivia Saunders had begun to disintegrate during the winter of 1935 at Anna Maria Key. Yet while there were signs that the marriage was breaking up, the writer and his wife found the quiet, un-

---

4. James Agee, *The Letters of James to Father Flye* (New York: George Braziller, 1962), October 30, 1934, p. 68, hereinafter cited in the text as *Letters* with date and page number.
5. Geneviève Moreau, *The Restless Journey of James Agee* (New York: William Morrow, 1977), 119, 120.
6. Fitzgerald, "A Memoir," 38.

complicated life off the Florida coast a welcome respite. Olivia, now Mrs. Robert Wood, remembers that, while Agee's days were filled with writing, her time was spent surf-casting and translating Gide.[7] In their twenty-dollar-a-month shack on the beach the Agees enjoyed the absence of social life. Olivia found the change from New York invigorating, and she was pleased to have her husband away from the "satellites," as she called them—Agee's admiring coterie who monopolized precious hours of his time in conversation.

While Olivia felt "really married for the first time" away from the friends and acquaintances who drifted in and out of their New York apartment, there was an undercurrent of tension during the winter at Anna Maria. Olivia recalls that her desire for a child, which Agee did not share, made him "very restless with me." This pulling in different directions ultimately produced a great strain on their relationship. Olivia remembers arguments when the novelist "would throw things and yell . . . and put on scenes." Their life together was also marred by Agee's depressions, during which he frequently spoke of his despair of ever becoming a "*great* writer." "I'm no good," he would often say. "I'll never amount to anything."[8]

Olivia was not surprised when the marriage began to fall apart. "I never saw us as grandparents," she says, "and never saw it [the marriage] as an enduring thing." When they were courting in Cambridge, she viewed Jim Agee and herself as young romantics, too much in love not to be married. Dwight Macdonald believes that Agee's marriage to Olivia grew out of affection for her family, and particularly for her father.[9]

The young writer was obviously attracted to the cultivated, close-knit feeling of the Saunders' home. "My parents were extraordinarily stimulating," Olivia Wood says of Dr. and Mrs. Saunders. They were deeply interested in young people and were much taken by Agee's "tremendous charm" and his intellectual sophistication. Dr. Saun-

7. Olivia S. Wood, interview, March 22, 1977.
8. *Ibid.*
9. *Ibid.*; Macdonald, interview, December 30, 1976.

58

ders, professor of chemistry at Hamilton College and a gracious and musically talented individual, was warmly congenial with his son-in-law. Olivia Wood acknowledged the deep bond between the two men and says of Jim: "He had an enormous feeling about my father." The young man was particularly struck by the way Dr. Saunders lived, his daughter remembers: "Jim said that my father reminded him of his grandfather." In the "Dream Sequence" chapter written for *A Death in the Family*, Agee could well have had Dr. Saunders and Joel Tyler (among others) in mind: "In every older man, constantly, he had looked for a father." [10]

The strong affection that James Agee had for the Saunders' family did not prevent his growing apart from Olivia. The prospect of divorce, however, deeply pained the writer, and Robert Fitzgerald wrote of "months of indecisions and revisions and colloquies over the parting with Via." The idea of his wife's being alone and without funds (alimony was out of the question) produced "great guilt" in Agee, according to Olivia. [11]

Before the separation, however, Agee was seeing Alma Mailman, Via's violin teacher and a member of Dr. Saunders' string quartet. Agee's guilt in the midst of this awkward situation protracted the dissolution of the first marriage. "He made it much too complicated," Olivia says of her parting with Jim. Agee once told Father Flye, with characteristic ambivalence, that he wished he could be married to Via and Alma at the same time. Agee and Via finally separated in December of 1937. In a 1938 letter to Dwight Macdonald, Agee wrote from Frenchtown, New Jersey, of the turbulence of his personal and professional life, "As you may have wind of, Via and I are divorcing. I am here with Alma Mailman whom you may but more likely do not know. I am at last, after some strained and chaotic months, getting to work on the tenant book." [12]

10. Wood, interview, March 22, 1977; James Agee, "A Death in the Family," (autograph working draft, in Humanities Research Center, University of Texas at Austin).

11. Fitzgerald, "A Memoir," 36; Wood, interview, March 22, 1977.

12. Wood, interview, March 22, 1977; James H. Flye, interview, December 28, 1976; James Agee to Dwight Macdonald, May 3, 1938, in possession of Macdonald, New York.

The sense of "terrific personal responsibility" that Agee felt about *Let Us Now Praise Famous Men* had moved him to write thousands of words about that summer. Henry Luce, his editor at *Fortune*, found it impossible to condense Agee's text of the Alabama assignment for publication in the magazine. After a year of deliberations between author and publisher, the manuscript and photographs were leased to Agee and Evans. Agee then decided to expand his contribution into a book-length work.

After Jim and Alma moved to a small frame house at 27 Second Street in Frenchtown, a contract was arranged with Harper to publish the tenant material in book form. Agee set about revising and drawing together the manuscript. He worked laboriously in his miniscule, sharpened-pencil script through that summer. Alma Agee Neuman speaks mystically of their early relationship in the mid-thirties: "He recognized a religiousness in me. . . . It was like two people trembling with each other; a lasting meeting of eyes." [13]

Robert Fitzgerald recalled that Agee was interested in getting criticism of his work during the months in Frenchtown. He often read drafts of the manuscript to friends. Of those sessions Fitzgerald wrote: "There isn't a word in *Let Us Now Praise Famous Men* that he— and I and others—did not ponder many times." Despite feverish rewrites of the text, the writer found his psychological problems menacing and work difficult. In July, 1938, Agee complained to Walker Evans, "Several times a day it becomes physically impossible to sit and write even through another sentence: and having stood up and walked around it is hard to get back into as (for me) stepping into a cold bath is . . . if the cold bath were also hot oil. The only way to do it seems to be . . . mindlessly." In the same letter, Agee wrote that it was "very annoying and disturbing" that he couldn't "be pulling and eager to take hold of the work." A feeling of self-doubt loomed in his mind as he further speculated that something was "damned seriously wrong" since he couldn't get over his writer's block. He unconvinc-

13. Alma Neuman, interview, March 21, 1977.

ingly attributed it to a lack of talent: "Probably . . . I'm mistaken in thinking I should try to write on Art at all, I don't know." [14]

Agee's correspondence of 1938 reveals a reawakening of interest in Freudian psychology, which he had explored in detail two years earlier at Anna Maria Key. In a May letter to Macdonald, he asked: "Have you any nonliterary books you could recommend or still better loan me, particularly on Viennese psychology?" After receiving his friend's recommendation of a book, Agee thanked him for it in a subsequent letter, adding, "I've got it and am halfway through puberty. He is quite a man, quite a man." The young writer resumed his earlier interest in recording his dreams as well. This practice apparently also stemmed from the winter at Anna Maria. During that period, Agee had read a book by a Jungian analyst, Frances Gillespy Wickes, *The Inner World of Childhood*, which contained two chapters on dreams and an introduction by Carl Jung. "Jim thought it was perfectly wonderful," Olivia remembers. At the conclusion of a letter to Walker Evans in August of the same year, Agee employed haunting images laced with humor: "A wonderful dream last night. Faulkner, martians, libraries, communism, and wilderness all mixed up in it; communism represented by a troop of singing girl scouts passing out leaflets in mimeographed rhyme. Late in the dream a large tract of wilderness lifted itself in a long sea wave, wet green on crest, red clay underneath, and lounged and folded over a quarter mile, suffocating me and all creation; yet as it sank I persisted." [15]

Agee had always been fascinated by the inner workings of the mind. He once told Mia that at age fourteen he had wanted to be an analyst. [16] Agee read psychology not simply to intellectualize about it, but for its application to himself. "Psychiatry, and for that matter

14. Fitzgerald, "A Memoir," 37; James Agee to Walker Evans, July 1, 1938, in Humanities Research Center, University of Texas at Austin.
15. Agee to Macdonald, May 3, 1938, Agee to Macdonald [1938], both in possession of Macdonald; Wood, interview; Agee to Evans [August 24, 1938], in Humanities Research Center, University of Texas at Austin.
16. Mia Agee, interview, March 24, 1977.

psychoanalysis still more," he wrote to Father Flye, "interest me intensely. . . . I realize that I have an enormously strong drive, on a universally broad front, toward self-destruction; and that I know little if anything about its sources or control" (September 21, 1941, *Letters*, 127).

The writer's mental difficulties were compounded by his profligate life-style and constant money worries. An obscenity-filled note to Evans in late July pointed to his continued sexual involvements. "I don't like the language of this letter," he concluded, "it may be partly explained by the act that I had last night [*sic*] hour of sexual nightmare whose locale was the Fortune office." The writer's proclivity for heterosexual encounters remained a strong motif during his adult life. "He had a great impact on women," David McDowell recalls. "They were drawn to him like moths to the flame."[17] Agee's sexual relationships, however, were characterized by a quality of honesty and openness. He remained remarkably candid with his wives, for example, about his infidelity and was tolerant—if not encouraging—of such liaisons in general. A case in point was the writer's attempt to link Alma and Walker Evans.

Agee's letters to Evans during the period frequently implored him to come to Frenchtown for a visit. Finally, in a note of early August, 1938, Agee wrote that he had a "disturbing feeling" about his friend's failure to come, that he believed Evans was "avoiding doing so." Jim addressed the problem indirectly: "I think I would know why, and can remember your talking of it some a month or five weeks ago." The "uneasy feeling of estrangement" stemmed from the mutual antagonism between Alma and Walker. Alma believes that Walker Evans, who "loved Jim and had a great respect for Jim's art," saw her as a threat to his writing. So bothered was the writer by the bad feeling between his wife-to-be and his close colleague that he encouraged Alma and Evans to develop a sexual relationship in the hope that it would forge a bond of friendship. Agee openly discussed this

17. Agee to Evans, July 27, 1938, in Humanities Research Center, University of Texas at Austin; David McDowell, interview, December 30, 1976.

situation in a later note to Evans: "I have caused each of you a certain amount of bother and am of course sorry. . . . However much or in whatever ways you happened to like each other, Good: I am enough of an infant, homosexual or post-dostoevskian to be glad. . . . I am enough a "man" not to care nor to think particularly whether I care or not. In whatever case, I recognize it as utterly irrelevant to any action or wishes of mine, whatever is of more meaning in it is also irrelevant to my existence." The proposed union between the writer's fiancée and the photographer never occurred.[18]

In addition to the tensions between Alma and Walker, the Frenchtown letters point to mutual discouragement on the part of the writer and his future wife. Agee quoted a friend's question to Alma, "What *do* you do all day?" in a September letter to the photographer. By way of explanation, he wrote of his intended, "She has her money from her family and so of course cannot drop her maid nor get a job. And so of course cannot drop the money and her family. She is pretty unhappy. I at the same time have sympathy with and pity for them and am incapable of either."[19]

A letter approximately a week later is revealing of Agee's mental state: "It is very painful, in a deadening way, to keep on feeling no excitement or vitality about work." Indeed, the majority of letters to Evans and Father Flye during this time sound a common theme of despair summed up by the writer's August "greeting" to the photographer: "I am not having a very good time." Mia Agee theorizes that what lay behind the writer's "tendency toward self-pity" was his early religious training and decided poetic propensity—primary factors in developing his "tragic" view of life.[20]

Even as Agee was never really able to get out from under his mor-

18. Agee to Evans, August 11, 1938, Humanities Research Center, University of Texas at Austin; Neuman, interview, March 21, 1977; Agee to Evans, n.d., in Humanities Research Center, University of Texas at Austin.
19. Agee to Evans [September 5, 1938], Humanities Research Center, University of Texas at Austin.
20. Agee to Evans, September 13, 14, August 11, 1938, all in Humanities Research Center, University of Texas at Austin; Mia Agee with Gerald Locklin, "Faint Lines," 159–60.

bidly intense introspection, he was always burdened with financial problems. Robert Fitzgerald's "Memoir" tells of finding a journal of Jim's that noted that, after the rent was paid on December 1 (1938), he would have $12.50 to his name; "in the same breath" he went on with plans for his marriage to Alma later that month.[21] The *Fortune* assignment on Brooklyn averted financial disaster, however, after the first of the year. But the succeeding months after Jim and Alma moved to a Brooklyn flat were difficult, as he wrote Father Flye: "It has been a very bad three months here in New York, full of a good many kinds of anxieties, money, rent and 'psychological' in me. I'm pulled apart between them so that I'm seldom good for much, but they are clearing now I think" ([June 27, 1939], *Letters*, 116).

The Agees returned to Frenchtown at the beginning of the summer, and the manuscript, "Three Tenant Families," was at Harper. By August, the writer's money situation reached a crisis point: "Because of lack of money, I am these days more temperate than I want to feel or be" ([August 10, 1939], *Letters*, 118). Problems with Harper soon developed. The Alabama assignment was a timely topic when it was first proposed, but since that time sharecroppers had been portrayed in dramas, documentary films, books, and photographs. "The sharecropper was at the center of the thirties."[22] By the end of the decade, however, the effects of the Depression had been felt for some time, and the tenant book was dated. In addition, Harper wanted Agee to make some manuscript changes. They deferred payment, but Agee would not agree to the changes. The writer was badly in debt when he appealed to Evans for funds in September: "More delay from Harpers leaves me again without a cent (or I have $3 now) and because I can't stand asking the same people I've been asking again I'm now asking you: could you loan me anything until (supposedly within a

21. Fitzgerald, "A Memoir," 41–42.
22. William Stott, *Let Us Now Praise Famous Men* panel discussion transcript, James Agee Memorial Library, St. Andrew's School, 55.

few days now) money comes through from Harpers. . . . Nice day but no clean clothes." [23]

The difficulties with the publishers, financial concerns, his relationship with Alma, and his lack of understanding about himself, brought the writer to a low mental state. "I am personally confused," Agee wrote Father Flye, "by my own definition of what ought to be; am frequently a bad artist, impure of heart, and an immoral man" (August 10, 1939, *Letters*, 118). As he did during other particularly bad periods, the writer turned confessionally to the priest, drowning as he was in despair and self-loathing: "I therefore feel cold, sick, vindictive, powerless and guilty against the world and between the wish to take vengeance on myself and on Harpers and "the world," and the wish to do the best I can, and feelings of hopeless coldness and incompetence, I can't even feel much anger, far less anything better. This may change. I hope it does, for I am drawing in to a dead point" (August 29 [1939], *Letters*, 122). He added, with macabre humor born of mental torment, "I'd be very glad of a person I could trust (and afford) to do mental surgery on me, and far more glad to grow up and need so much pother" (*Letters*, 121–22). In this letter, Agee's strong awareness of time passing was combined with his desire for further self-discipline: "Meanwhile I am thirty and have missed irretrievably all the trains I should have caught" (*Letters*, 122).

It is clear from this 1939 letter that James Agee knew that he wanted stability and permanence but felt that he was incapable of achieving them. The duality implicit in the writer's speaking about the need to take care of himself and his behaving otherwise is a tension which informed his life-style and letters. In a note written to Father Flye in December of that year, Agee expressed the filial bond that he felt between the priest, his wife, and himself during this difficult period: "I think I probably reach out toward you all and towards the Catholic faith as towards parents and wisdom and peace and my

23. Agee to Evans, September 8, 1939, in Humanities Research Center, University of Texas at Austin.

childhood. That may be a weak and panicked thing to do but that may not be a bad idea of itself" (December 26, [1939], *Letters*, 122–23). The writer's readings in Freudian psychology and Jungian psychoanalysis gave him the desire to explore his own psyche, but he expressed disenchantment with intellectualization not coupled with prudent action: "there is such a thing too as learning enough when you're half drowned to come in out of the rain" (*Letters*, 123).

In the spring of 1940, Jim and Alma, facing desperate financial problems, learned that Alma was pregnant. Negotiations at Harper were still deadlocked, so Robert Fitzgerald secured a job for his friend reviewing books at *Time*. Agee and Fitzgerald shared an office in what was then the new Time and Life Building for a year. The baby, Joel, arrived in March of 1940 and, according to Alma, was named for Agee's grandfather.

In the meantime, the Agees had moved once again, this time to a place on West Fifteenth Street. It was during this period of grueling writing projects that Harper finally gave back (after a year and a half) the manuscript, "Three Tenant Families." Shortly afterward Houghton-Mifflin accepted it. Agee was, of course, relieved to have found a publisher and expressed the desire "to be through with it." In a letter of December, 1940, he wrote to Fitzgerald that the book was due to come out after the first of the year and added, "I now thoroughly regret using the subtitle (Let Us Now Praise Famous Men) as I should never have forgotten I would. I am rather anxious to look at it, finished and in print—possibly, also, to read it in that form—but I have an idea I'll be unable to stand to." [24]

The publication date was deferred, however, while Agee spent time correcting page proofs. *Let Us Now Praise Famous Men* was finally issued in the fall of 1941. In his reply to Father Flye's comments on the work, the thirty-one-year-old Agee was consumed with self-doubt, believing he had compromised the sharecroppers' dignity. He called *Famous Men* "a sinful book at least in all degrees . . . 'falling

24. Fitzgerald, "A Memoir," 44.

short of the mark' and . . . in more corrupt ways as well" ([September 25, 1941], *Letters*, 128).

Critical reaction to the book was varied. Most reviewers agreed with Erik Wensberg's 1960 reappraisal of it as "a variegated work resembling in its form nothing else in American letters." A number of critics, including Lionel Trilling, felt that *Famous Men* was a failure of "moral realism." Trilling questioned Agee's "inability to see these people as anything but good." His uncritical stance, Trilling suggested, produced out-of-control guilt in the writer which obscured "the truth that poverty and suffering are not in themselves virtue." Despite his reservations about the author's objectivity, however, Trilling called the text "the most realistic and important moral effort of our American generation."[25]

Several reviews observed that Agee's deep empathy and sense of commitment to the tenants created stylistic problems in the work. Agee's overanxious attempt to "get his story" had, the critics felt, resulted in sections that were uneven, rambling, and jumbled in their view. Alan Holder, in siding with Lionel Trilling, wrote that the experience had aroused a torrent of subjective pity and compassion within Agee that was as indulgent as it was boundless. In a 1966 article on the work, Holder stated that the writer "set himself up as a kind of moral lightning-rod to divert the shocks of judgment away from his tenants, receiving them upon his own head." In a curious way, the critics sensed victory in the midst of thorny thematic and point-of-view issues. An unsigned *Time* review of 1941 called *Famous Men* "the most distinguished failure of the season," incorporating "some of the most exciting U.S. prose since Melville."[26]

In October, with the publication of the book at last a reality, Agee

25. Erik Wensberg, "Celebration, Adoration, and Wonder," *Nation*, November 26, 1960, p. 418; Lionel Trilling, "Greatness with One Fault in It," *Kenyon Review*, IV (Winter, 1942), 102.
26. Alan Holder, "Encounter in Alabama: Agee and the Tenant Farmer," *Virginia Quarterly Review*, XLII (Spring, 1966), 199; Review of *Let Us Now Praise Famous Men*, in *Time*, October 13, 1941, p. 104.

settled into reviewing films for *Time*. He and Alma moved once again, this time to a place on Bleeker Street. By the winter, the marriage had disintegrated: "Alma is in Mexico—so is Joel—nominally, presumably, perhaps very probably, that is broken forever." The break had been prefigured in a December letter to Fitzgerald in which he spoke of his "exceedingly quiet marriage"—a union that he said could be glorious but was in the main not true to his way of operating or to his personality.[27]

Following his break with Alma, Jim signed on as film reviewer for *Nation* in December, 1942—a post which he held until September, 1948. In the autumn of 1945, Agee married Mia Fritsch, an Austrian-born staff worker whom he had known at *Fortune*. In November, 1946, their first daughter, Julia Teresa, was born.

During the period when his first two children were born, Agee was feeling the need to come to terms with his mortality. His preoccupation with death, which was an active part of his suicidal fantasies, took on a different shape during this period. The writer was keenly aware of the passage of time and of the inevitable end of his own life. He wrote to Father Flye on his birthday in November, 1945, "So I am now 36. For days I have had premonitions: more solemn than any in years. . . . There are premonitions I superstitiously fear to write but will: 1) I will die during this year, unexpectedly (parallel to my father's death at just that age); 2) I will be killed after long torture, by one or another kind of enemy. . . . This is cheap drunken talk; but also, sober too, I mean it" (November 27, 1945, *Letters*, 154). Agee expected to die in the manner of his father ("unexpectedly") and to join him in death at precisely the same age. Mia Agee corroborates the depth of her husband's premonition, saying that he was "convinced" of it. "Getting him through thirty-six," she adds, "was really something."[28] Agee, obviously, did not die during that year, but from that point on, suffered similar forebodings at certain periods and events. An appendectomy in the spring of 1948 re-

27. Fitzgerald, "A Memoir," 46, 49.
28. Mia Agee, interview, March 24, 1977.

awakened those difficult emotions. About the operation, he said he felt "a sense of death," and afterwards he wrote the priest that "late the night before it, in the hospital, I felt very grave about it." He mentioned that he had written "Mia a long letter, including messages to friends," and had carefully placed it where it would not be lost, "in case I didn't come through it" ([April 10, 1948], *Letters*, 173).

The depression that accompanied the death fantasies was hardly new to Agee, but he was able to handle it more maturely. During the thirties Agee's solution to his serious mental and marital lows was suicide. Eventually, though, Agee was able to replace his desperate, end-it-all attitude with the belief shared by Robert Frost's proverb-quoting housekeeper in "A Servant to Servants": "The best way out is always through." [29] In a letter to Father Flye in the spring of 1949, the author chronicled his mental condition and gave his prognosis: "This has certainly been as bad an eight months for me as I can remember. I feel phases of something different from my ordinary depressions and apathy: more like galloping melancholia. My confidence and hope are very low and at times non-existent. Yet in general I feel I just have to wait it out . . . if I manage to wait those bad stretches out, I will come through all right" (May 4, 1949, *Letters*, 178–79).

While James Agee worked as never before to live with and understand himself psychologically, there is evidence to indicate that he also wanted to come to terms with himself spiritually. The preoccupying thoughts of death may well have prompted him to wonder at the nature of his soul and his own religiousness. In a note to the priest written in March, 1948, he closed with "God bless you," and then added as a kind of postscript, "But will you please tell me: are you in any way offended that I, who don't even know most of the time, whether I believe in God, should say that? I realize my lack of right to, but I believe in obeying a thing which is spontaneous" ([March 2, 1948], *Letters*, 171–72). Agee then asked, in the most direct way, for

29. Edward Connery Lathem (ed.), *The Collected Poetry of Robert Frost* (New York: Holt, Rinehart, and Winston, 1969), 64.

69

the priest's guidance, "Will you tell me and, if you see any way to, 'advise' me in general? I am concerned to try to clarify my belief or unbelief" (*Letters*, 172). Father Flye, in his reply on April 4, offered benediction, perhaps the hoped-for response behind the writer's question, by way of his answer: "You asked if I feel somewhat incongruous to have you use such an expression as 'God bless you.' I certainly do not. You are naturally religious. Some persons have a fundamental sense of reverence and of tenderness, basic qualities in religion, and of such are you" (April 4, 1948, *Letters*, 172).

Despite Father Flye's approval of the writer's "naturally religious" qualities, it is obvious that the tension which Agee felt about his faith was a recurrent problem. As was characteristic of so much in his life, he felt unable—whether out of superstitious fear or for deeper psychological reasons—to embrace religion, or anything, in its totality. The duality of this part of his life shocked him, but he could not bring the disparate attitudes together: "It seems incredible to me," he wrote Father Flye on "Early Maundy Thursday" in 1945, "not to be a Christian and a Catholic in the simplest and strictest sense of the words" ([March 29, 1945], *Letters*, 139). Yet, for him, another course was not possible: "I am at once grateful for the emotions and doubtful of them" (*Letters*, 139).

In addition to his increasingly frequent mention of spiritual concerns in the letters to the priest, "another fact which contributed to Agee's growing religious awareness," Victor Kramer suggests, was his trip to the Saint Andrew's campus in 1949. The writer returned to the school in February of that year for about a week to visit his dying stepfather, Father Erskine Wright. The long estrangement between the two was ended, Mia Agee remembers, when Agee went to the priest's bedside: "They made peace when Jim went down there." Mrs. Clyde Medford, the family friend and night nurse who cared for Father Wright in his last illness, recalls the night the priest died: "Rufus came rushing down and said, 'Mrs. Medford, will you come right quick? We think Father is dying.' I just rushed on up there with him. He just breathed a time or two after I got there. . . . Rufus just

70

fell down on his knees and started saying some prayers."[30] The occasion of his stepfather's death and funeral at the place so hallowed in the writer's mind may well have caused him to think creatively about the scene of his formative religious instruction.

Following the visit to Saint Andrew's, Agee agreed to participate in a symposium, "Religion and the Intellectuals," sponsored by *Partisan Review* in February, 1950. In that article, the writer stated that he maintained a "religious consciousness," and he went on to explain that he regarded "man and human life" as sufficient inspiration to generate awe, compassion, and reverence. But Agee further qualified this statement, adding he suspected that for him "this consciousness is enhanced (perhaps created) by unconscious undertones of belief and semi-belief in God."[31]

The letters to Father Flye, particularly those written in the late 1940s, Agee's 1949 visit to Saint Andrew's, and his participation in the symposium on religion led Victor Kramer to conclude: "We know therefore that Agee had been seriously thinking about religious questions during the years preceding his decision to write *The Morning Watch*." It was shortly after the *Partisan Review* article was printed that the writer, in a burst of energy, wrote the draft of *The Morning Watch* in a week during the spring of 1950.[32]

The religious import of the Alabama experience for Agee may also have created a need to synthesize that vision with his own life experience. The long-range effect of the tenant experience was considerable—both artistically and personally. Alma Neuman recalls a return visit which she and the writer made to the Gudgers' home where Agee and Evans had lived. For Agee the day he and Alma spent there was "like coming home." Perhaps it was their visit that prompted the

30. Victor A. Kramer, "'Religion at Its Deepest Intensity': The Stasis of Agee's *The Morning Watch*," *Renascence*, XXVII (Summer, 1975), 222; Mia Agee, interview, March 24, 1977; Mrs. Clyde Medford, interview, December 14, 1976.
31. James Agee, "Religion and the Intellectuals," *Partisan Review*, XVII (February, 1950), 112.
32. Kramer, "Religion at its Deepest Intensity," 223; Agee mentions that he wrote *The Morning Watch* in a week in a letter to Father Flye, (May 23 [1950], *Letters*, 181).

adult Agee to focus on the forces and influences that had moved him and stirred his imagination as a boy and had culminated in *Famous Men*. *The Morning Watch*, while it marked a radical departure from the style and technique of the earlier work, provided a thematic continuation of *Famous Men*. "There is fine contrapuntal playing of profane against sacred motifs," the writer said of his first extended piece of fiction. Beyond the aesthetic pleasure that *The Morning Watch* gave him, the real attraction in writing it was personal: "Agee was using fiction, quite clearly, to investigate his own past."[33]

The seeds for Agee's story of a young boy's search for identity at a mountain boarding school were obviously sown in his own childhood. The author's plan for the novella makes clear his intention to render his years at Saint Andrew's authentically. In May of 1950 Agee wrote to Father Flye:

> I've been wanting by the way to ask your help on a few points, some for the story, some for the book: What time, about, is just daylight, *Standard* Time, at St. Andrew's in early April (say April 1) and around April 12? And (as of Knoxville, there can't be much difference), what time is the beginning of dusk, "sunset," full darkness on May 18? And what time is *sunrise* at St. Andrew's, April 1 and 12? And just sunlight, May 18? Just roughly standard time in all cases. (May 23, 1950, *Letters*, 181)

In a footnote to this letter, Father Flye has stated that the story Agee was working on was "Undirectable Director," a piece about John Huston, and the book was *The Morning Watch*. The priest insists that the material in the novella is virtual autobiography: "The scene of *The Morning Watch*—the dormitory, the Maundy Thursday Watch in relays through the night before the Blessed Sacrament—is unmistakably Saint Andrew's, and the originals of probably all the characters

33. Durant da Ponte, "James Agee: The Quest for Identity," *Tennessee Studies in Literature*, VIII (Winter, 1963), 32; W. M. Frohock, "James Agee: The Question of Unkept Promise," *Southwest Review*, XLII (Summer, 1957), 228.

in that story would be easily recognizable by anyone familiar with that place in the early 1920's." [34]

Flye's assessment is supported by Agee's classmates. William Peyton, a Saint Andrew's alumnus (class of 1926) who was portrayed as Undertaker, the "giant sad boy" described in the novella, wrote, "At the time of writing this story, Rufus Agee was living his life over again at St. Andrew's." Another alumnus of 1926, Edmund J. Phillips, agreed: "I took, on first reading, the entire action—other than Rufus' religious celebration—to be 100% true." [35]

That Rufus Agee should have chosen to write a book about his alma mater is not surprising. The school was the center of his existence and, because of Father and Mrs. Flye, a spiritual home, a refuge removed from the cares of the world. In his essay, "The Turning Point," David McDowell recalled the visit which Jim and Via made to Saint Andrew's in mid-April, 1936, following the winter at Anna Maria. Although at the time of the visit McDowell was about to graduate from the school and had never met Agee, he wrote, "I felt I already knew him, for he was the 'Rufus' I had heard so much about since I was thirteen." The schoolboy had learned of the writer from the Saint Andrew's faculty and staff, chiefly from Father and Mrs. Flye, "his dearest friends and mentors." [36]

Jim and David spent many hours hiking through the woods, talking about poetry, and playing fierce games of tennis. The young McDowell immediately sensed the hold that Sewanee Mountain had upon his companion. The two of them occasionally walked out to Piney Point, a cliff that opens out onto a wide, incredibly beautiful vista. Jim told David, "perhaps at Piney Point," that the area "was his favorite part of the world." [37]

34. James H. Flye, "An Article of Faith," *Harvard Advocate*, CV (February, 1972), 21.
35. James Agee, *The Morning Watch* (Boston: Houghton-Mifflin, 1951), 18, hereinafter cited in the text as *TMW* with page number; William Peyton to Walter B. Chambers, November 29, 1972, Edmund J. Phillips to Chambers [1972], both in James Agee Memorial Library, St. Andrew's School.
36. David McDowell, "The Turning Point," in David Madden (ed.), *Remembering James Agee* (Baton Rouge: Louisiana State University Press, 1974), 95.
37. *Ibid.*, 97.

73

The month Jim Agee spent in middle Tennessee provided a regrounding of experience for the novella to come. McDowell notes that his friend "especially wanted to retrace his steps to the Sand Cut, an abandoned sand quarry now, as then, deep and filled with water." The Sand Cut, referred to by name in *The Morning Watch*, is the place to which Richard and his companions escape for a swim during the Lenten watch. "The Sand Cut was the forbidden territory," Charles May has written, "and Richard's route there after the watch took him across the same grounds that one may still trace today, from the same Lady Chapel, across the same Mountain Goat railroad tracks to the same forbidden swimming hole." [38]

While the Sand Cut during Agee's years at Saint Andrew's was visited regularly by the students, permission had to be obtained from the master of the day. There is no evidence to document the particular incident described in *The Morning Watch*, but William Peyton thought it "very likely" that Rufus could have made an unauthorized visit to the quarry. Edmund Phillips concurred: "I am sure he would," he stated, "Rufus would do anything." The Sand Cut, then, was a familiar, popular spot frequented by Saint Andrew's boys. McDowell said of the 1936 trip he and Agee took to the swimming hole: "He made no mention of it in any literary way, but I am sure he was touching base with some of the memories and perceptions that would later be used so well in *The Morning Watch*." [39]

Once the idea for a story became more clear, Agee found himself beset by the usual self-doubt. On a sheet headed "Notes," the writer indicated that the style and plot had become slippery: "Is this worth doing? I can't get any solid hold of it or confidence in it. A much gentler way of seeing it and writing it? Or more casual? Mine is very dry and very literary." [40]

38. McDowell, "The Turning Point," 97; Charles W. Mayo, "James Agee: His Literary Life and Work" (Ph.D. dissertation, George Peabody college, 1969), 238.

39. Peyton to Chambers, November 29, 1972, Phillips to Chambers [1972], both in Agee Library, McDowell, "The Turning Point," 96.

40. James Agee, "The Morning Watch" (incomplete manuscript drafts and notes in Humanities Research Center, University of Texas at Austin).

Agee centered the novella around the Maundy Thursday morning watch observed during Lent at Saint Andrew's. Because he feared that the practice would seem arcane and esoteric to the general reader, Agee included a prefatory comment to the work. There was a note appended to this long and, finally, unused passage, which was obviously meant for an editor: "If the opening of the story seems too unclear, the following can be inserted before the beginning of the story as it now stands." A portion of this excised material is particularly noteworthy:

> Between the middle of the morning on Maundy Thursday and the Mass of the Presanctified Good Friday morning the Blessed Sacrament was exposed in the Lady Chapel and the boys, teachers and priests of the School, and some of the people who lived nearby on the Mountain, signed the list on the bulletin board for half-hour periods in the continuous watch that was kept before it. Since there was no compulsion, even of an invisible kind, it is probable that most of those who signed and watched were sincerely devout (though some signed perhaps ostentatiously often); but since no hour was forbidden to anyone, except through conflict of classes or other obligations, and since the opportunities for keeping irregular hours were particularly rare for the younger boys, the hours between midnight and daybreak were crowded with their semi-legible signatures. [41]

This introductory section is valuable for an understanding of how faithful the novella is to Agee's actual experiences. The Lady Chapel, a small side chapel off the nave of the Saint Andrew's Chapel, was used during the writer's matriculation for the Lenten watch observance and is still so used today. Edmund Phillips has written that the schedule of times was posted on a bulletin board "near [the] entrance of [the] old Saint Andrew's building." Students, faculty members, and townspeople, as Agee suggests, would sign up, generally for thirty

41. James Agee, "The Morning Watch" (note, in Humanities Research Center, University of Texas at Austin).

minutes. The system of rotation used at the school was authentically retold in the book, according to William Peyton: "The Maunday-Thursday [sic] setting is true. The boys being called all through the night, to relieve those on watch."[42]

The school in the novella is clearly Saint Andrew's, transcribed literally, and in the same way, Richard, the novella's protagonist, is a depiction of Rufus Agee as a boy. The opening of the work is a nostalgic recollection of the dormitory milieu Agee had known. He intended the autobiographical material in this reverie about his boyhood to be "deeply evocative," noting that "R's waking emotion and the hollowness of the dormitory bed must be as nearly immediate and simultaneous as possible." Agee bestowed on Richard the nickname that had been given him at Saint Andrew's and gave him a bright, intuitive personality at odds with the antiintellectual environment of the school. John Stroup, a classmate of Agee's, recognized this conflict between Richard and the world around him as Agee's "attempt to represent himself—intelligent, sensitive, precocious—" in the rugged Saint Andrew's milieu. William Peyton described the novella as "the memory of the influence of his [Rufus'] playmates ever in conflict with his religious education." Perhaps most revealing of the author's faithfulness to life on the mountain is a working note in which he listed classmates and priests at the school in one column and their fictional counterparts in another.

> Dave Mooney—Hobe Gillum
> Raymond Kersey—Jimmy Toole
> Bob Stewart—George Fitzgerald
> Paul Green—Claude Grey
> Deaconess Barbour—Deaconess Spenser
> Fr. Whitall—Fr. Whitman
> Fr. Flye—Fr. Fish
> Fr. Lorey—Fr. Weiler

42. Phillips to Chambers [1972], Peyton to Chambers, November 29, 1972, both in Agee Library.

Fr. Orum—Fr. Ogle
Fr. Campbell—Fr. McPhitridge [43]

Not surprisingly, *The Morning Watch* created intense speculation among Saint Andrew's faculty, students, and alumni as to the characters' identities. In parallel lists composed by Phillips and Peyton, there was virtually no dispute about the major characters. Of his several conversations with Father Flye about the book, Edmund Phillips commented: "He told me who several were and we would guess at others. Some are obvious, some are likely, and some have probability."[44]

Among those figures who are clearly modeled after Saint Andrew's personages is Willard Rivenburg, the stand-in for Clarence Lautzenheiser. During the watch in the novella, Richard and a few of the smaller boys are startled to see "the reckless primitive profile and the slash-lined blue-black cheek of the great athlete Willard Rivenburg, whom they had never seen in quite such quiet intimacy" (*TMW*, 20). A Saint Andrew's alumnus characterized "Lautzy" as an "all-around athlete" and "the pride and joy of St. A. in an athletic sense at that time."[45]

As Richard studies Willard, who, like Lautzy was considerably older than the other students, he feels a deep joy at his proximity to this celebrated local figure, the possessor of an "almost magical quality" in athletics. "He began to feel," Agee wrote, "a sense of honor and privilege in having this surprising chance to be so near to him and to watch him so closely, to really see him" (*TMW*, 22). The novelist's almost worshipful description of the sports figure is revealing. Lautzenheiser, who used tobacco and swore convincingly, was a symbol to the young Agee of masculine prowess and independence.

43. Agee, "The Morning Watch" (incomplete manuscript drafts and notes); Mayo, "James Agee," 244; Peyton to Chambers, November.29, 1972, in Agee Library; Agee, "The Morning Watch" (incomplete manuscript drafts and notes).
44. Phillips to Chambers [1972], in Agee Library.
45. Peyton to Chambers, November 29, 1972, in Agee Library.

TELL ME WHO I AM

In *The Morning Watch* Richard sounds the Ageean theme of sexual passivity and insecurity that will resurface in *A Death in the Family*, where Rufus longs to be recognized as a man in his father's eyes.

Another of the book's figures about whom there is no need to guess a prototype is that of Deaconess Spenser. The character of the deaconess was based on Deaconess Barbour, a teacher of business at Saint Andrew's. When Richard and several classmates misbehave slightly during their vigil, "he could hear the harsh whispered reprimand whistling through her false teeth" (*TMW*, 30). The deaconess was a forbidding figure with "her wattles a violent red and her mouth pulled in tight" (*TMW*, 30). Richard and the other boys are forewarned of her approach by the sound of "rustling starch" (*TMW*, 62). According to one of Deaconess Barbour's former students, Agee's characterization was appropriate: "She was as stiff, serious and severe as Rufus indicates." Another student recalled that Deaconess Barbour "was laced up so tight her face looked bloated." Her classes were marked by a fearfully quiet orderliness, and a withering glance from her brought many a daydreaming boy to attention. William Peyton recalled that "the small boys were afraid of her." [46]

The representation of Father Flye as Father Fish is also unmistakable. In his portrayal of his mentor, Agee used several of his actual experiences to describe the relationship between Richard and the priest. It is of the afternoon language lessons with Father Flye that he writes when Richard thinks, "with Father Fish's help he had learned several hundred words of French" (*TMW*, 23). In the midst of his meditation during the watch, Richard prays, "Blood of Christ inebriate me." He then digresses on the connotations of *inebriate*, a word of which he is fond—particularly for its general meaning of "to make drunk, to intoxicate" (*TMW*, 32). Thinking back to his looking the word up in the dictionary, Richard remembers that he had "asked Father Fish about it and Father Fish had shown him that it was possible to be amused by the word without feeling irreverent" (*TMW*, 32).

46. Phillips to Chambers [1972], Peyton to Chambers, November 29, 1972, both in Agee Library.

While Father Flye cannot recall whether or not Agee questioned him about *inebriate*, the spirit behind Fish's explanation to Richard that the ancients tended toward flamboyance in their prayers and that such expressions need not be taken literally is true to the quality of understanding between Flye and Agee.[47] Agee pointed to Father Flye's sterling sense of humor when he wrote of Richard's vague notion that Father Fish "had been as amused at him, as at the word" (*TMW*, 33).

It is of course interesting to speculate on the significance of the term *fish* in a work that is consciously symbolic. Of the five priests referred to in the novella, Father Fish is the only one whose surname is rich in religious symbolism. The fish was a symbol of Christ for the early Church. Agee's notes for the story indicate that he was well aware of the implicit meanings of the emblems used in the text ("The snake. Is he too obvious a symbol, and the locust?"[48]). Knowing the profound mixture of respect and affection that the writer had for Father Flye and realizing the abundant use of signs in the work, we may conclude that the surname *Fish* was consciously selected. Agee clearly saw Father Flye as a father-priest, an incarnation of God-in-man.

James Agee's conscious modeling of his fictional creations on his Saint Andrew's teachers and peers allowed him to put his early years into perspective and to do it with a new objectivity afforded by artistic distance. Agee's father and mother also figure in *The Morning Watch*. In one scene, as Richard enters the nave of the chapel, his awareness is at once stirred by the banks of spring flowers and mass of candles. The closed sanctuary, the fragrant blossoms, and the burning candle tallow make the air heavy with scent and call to Richard's mind the memory of his father's funeral. The words *God* and *death* merge in his consciousness and become one: "Dead, the word prevailed; and before him, still beyond all other stillness, he saw as freshly as six years before his father's prostrate head and, through the efforts to hide it, the mortal blue dent in the impatient chin" (*TMW*, 28).

47. James H. Flye, interview, March 24, 1977.
48. Agee, "The Morning Watch" (incomplete manuscript drafts and notes).

Twelve-year-old Richard's father had died when he was six just as James Agee's father had and just as Rufus Follett's father would in *A Death in the Family*. Richard prefigures Rufus and shares his view of the death, inasmuch as Rufus in the aftermath of Jay Follett's funeral "said to himself, over and over, 'Dead. Dead.'" Richard's memory of his father's body lying "still beyond all other stillness" is parallel to Rufus' last look at his father: "Rufus had never known such stillness."[49] (*ADF*, 307). The "impatient chin" which Richard remembers echoes Agee's description of Jay Follett's "look of impatience, the chin strained a little upward" (*ADF*, 307). The "mortal blue dent" passage in *The Morning Watch* is analogous to the description in *A Death in the Family*: "At the exact point of the chin, there was [a] small blue mark" (*ADF*, 308). Finally, in his study of the two works, Charles Mayo was struck by Richard's mother and Rufus' mother explaining the father's death in the same way. In *The Morning Watch*, Richard's mother tells him, "Daddy was terribly hurt so God has taken him up to heaven to be with Him and he won't come back to us ever any more" (*TMW*, 120). In *A Death in the Family*, she says, "Daddy didn't come home. He isn't going to come ever any more. He's—gone away to heaven and he isn't ever coming home again" (*ADF*, 251).[50]

Both versions of the father's death were based closely on James Agee's recollections of his own father's death and funeral. In a sheaf of notes for *A Death in the Family* he recalled in precise detail how he had felt as a six-year-old on the morning of his father's rites. It appears from his comments that the bruise on Jay Agee's chin haunted him as a child and as an adult, for it was the only visible sign of what had caused Jay's demise. As an adult Jim Agee vividly remembered the coffin, his father's face, and the bruise "just under the point of the chin." Jay's chin, he noted, "looked strong and quiet, not swollen or in any way misshapen," but was "more conspicuous or focused be-

49. James Agee, *A Death in the Family* (New York: McDowell, Obolensky, 1957), 316, hereinafter cited in the text as *ADF* with page number.
50. Mayo, "James Agee," 238.

80

cause of the bruise." The bruise on the chin, the point of impact between his father's body and the car's steering wheel, was obviously the mark of death, and it haunted him: "Did someone, now or before or later, say, 'Not another mark on him'?"[51]

Apart from the authentic re-creation in Richard of his own feelings about his father's death, *The Morning Watch* is also noteworthy for the revealing passages about the hero's mother. Agee writes about the sense of separation Richard feels while "watching his mother's cottage, the one place he was almost never allowed to go, sometimes by the hour" (*TMW*, 41). In an illuminating juxtaposition, the passage about Richard's estrangement from his mother follows immediately the section about the joy of visiting Father's Fish's cottage ("friendliness was certain there"). William Peyton was aware of tension between the boy Agee and his mother. He described Laura Agee Wright as "a wonderful and God-fearing woman," who recognized that her son needed to be among boys his own age. Likewise, Richard's mother tells him, "mother thinks you need to be among other boys" (*TMW*, 42). Peyton wrote that Agee's mother had taught her son about the Church "since he was old enough to talk." But Rufus Agee's carefree mischievousness with his classmates, according to Peyton, "butted against" his mother's strong pietistic sense of discipline and "created a conflict" between mother and son. Peyton feels that their relationship is at the heart of the novella.[52]

While each of Agee's wives believes that the writer and his mother had a generally close relationship, each acknowledges a large difference between mother and son in temperament and lifestyle. James Agee's sister, Emma Agee Ling, observes that her mother "seemed to feel closer to Jim than he did to her." Richard's bitterness at not being allowed to go home was Rufus Agee's own experience at Saint Andrew's, according to Mia Agee. Her mother-in-law, says Mrs. Agee, obviously "thought she was doing the right thing," but

51. James Agee, "A Death in the Family" (notes and fragments of manuscript in Humanities Research Center, University of Texas at Austin).
52. Peyton to Chambers, November 29, 1972, in Agee Library.

the ban on seeing his mother created a strange and absurd situation. The boy Agee was "baffled" by the separation from his mother so soon after his father had deserted him in death. The estrangement from both parents led Rufus-Richard to feel, in Mia's words, "lonely and isolated." She speaks of Father Flye-Fish, who rescued the boy from this alien world, as "a lifesaver."[53]

Despite Laura Agee's hope that her son's education would be left to the priests and monks, the novella makes it clear that Rufus' tutelage was largely in his classmates' domain. Certainly Agee admired and envied the "manly, independent and self-assured behavior" of the few older students, like Clarence Lautzenheiser, at the school. The chasm that separated the Holy Cross Fathers from the students is a dialectic central to *The Morning Watch* and indicative of the conflicting forces within Richard-Rufus. Geneviève Moreau notes that "religious zeal was not rare at Saint Andrew's; it was a practice more or less imposed on the boys."[54] In *The Morning Watch* Richard sees "the tall ghostly moving" of Father Whitman's white habit, as the priest stops to waken Jimmy Toole, so that he can take his turn at the watch. When Father Whitman shakes the boy's shoulder, Jimmy snarls, "*Quit* it you God *damn*—"; and then with "servile Irish charm" says, "Aw sure Father, I din know it was *you* Father" (*TMW*, 6–7).

Agee's novella is a depiction of two worlds—sacred and profane—and a young boy's ambivalence as he is torn between them. The boy Richard's religious education is complex and varied. He is impressed by the rich vestments, the prayers and psalms, the ringing of the changes, the odors of flowers and incense. The religious instruction at the school has provided Richard-Rufus with "an elaborate Christian symbology," including Lent and Holy Week when the Lady Chapel is draped in purple, then black, as images of mourning;

53. Emma Agee Ling, telephone conversation, March 7, 1977; Mia Agee, interview, March 24, 1977.
54. Moreau, *The Restless Journey*, 48, 49.

the austere tabernacle, and the thick, luxuriant scents of burning candles.[55]

Rufus Agee, like his fictional counterpart, was an intellectual, unique to the Saint Andrew's community, who fashioned his own credo from the prophetic and prosaic influences around him. Although he became a seasoned skeptic in matters of faith and practice, Agee did cherish much of the piety and reverence he came to know at Saint Andrew's. The impact of this religious setting upon the writer was so considerable that in his notes for the novella, Agee wrote that the overall concern of the book was to be "Religion at its deepest intensity or clarity of childhood faith and emotions." Discussion of the thesis was to be accomplished by "the watching the Chapel; wanderings of the mind and efforts at prayer; memories of the dead father, imaginations of sex and sport; workings of guilt; excuses of religious intention and complications of guilt and pride; the excitement of emergence at about dawn . . . the walk through the woods to the swim.[56]

The emphasis on guilt is an important element in the story. As noted elsewhere, guilt was a live issue in the writer's personal life. Olivia Wood comments that Agee was "consumed with guilt— about everything." In *The Morning Watch*, Richard has anticipated for months the watch between Maundy Thursday and Good Friday. Victor Kramer has written that Richard "hoped to pray extremely well."[57] When he finds, instead, that his prayers are continually interrupted by daydreams and reveries, Richard believes he has failed. His inability to be devout at the apogee of religious feeling during the school and church year is the source of enormous guilt. The young boy makes desperate, abortive attempts to effect genuine religious emotion, mentally chronicling past efforts of penance and self-mortification. In a scene reminiscent of the spiritual panic of Stephen

55. *Ibid.*, 50.
56. Agee, "The Morning Watch" (incomplete manuscript drafts and notes).
57. Kramer, "'Religion at its Deepest Intensity,'" 221.

Dedalus, Richard recalls eating worms in the woods and the near-tasting of his own waste, while fantasizing about his own crucifixion (*TMW*, 44).

After Richard's second half-hour vigil with the same pattern of distraction, he gives up: "What he saw in his mind's eye was a dry chalice, an empty Grail" (*TMW*, 87). In his decision to join his classmates, Hobe and Jim, for a swim at the off-limits Sand Cut, Richard leaves the sacred world for the secular. Yet during the hike to the quarry, the hero is confronted by a variety of religious symbols. He finds a locust's shell (an emblem of death and suffering), hears a rooster's crow (betrayal), kills a snake (good and evil), and dives into, and reemerges from, a pool (rebirth).[58]

Significantly, it is in bathing in these waters that the hero is baptized, is resurrected. Richard breaks through the sense of loneliness that he—nicknamed Socrates—feels with his peers and is able to revel in the communion with his companions. For the first time, he is able to move beyond his repressed notions of religion by moving out into the world. Furthermore, says David Reishman, the novella suggests that as "Christ is attempting a reconciliation with his Father . . . the hero . . . experiences that same problem in his own life."[59] Like Richard, James Agee faced the difficult problem of reconciling himself with a father who was dead and a mother who *seemed* dead.

At the end of the novella, Richard thinks of the dead snake, "so far gone . . . beyond really feeling anything ever any more" (*TMW*, 170). He is thunderstruck by the phrase "ever any more" and recalls his mother's words at the time of his father's death, "and he won't come back to us ever any more." While the protagonist finds his mind easing as he walks back to the school, in the face of certain discipline, he cannot let go of the memory of his father's death. As Richard turns toward the main building, he is holding the locust shell dis-

58. Victor A. Kramer, "Agee: A Study of the Poetry, Prose, and Unpublished Manuscript," (Ph.D. dissertation, University of Texas, 1966), 96.
59. John Reishman, *The Morning Watch* panel discussion transcript, October 10, 1972, in James Agee Memorial Library, St. Andrew's School, 8.

covered earlier, which becomes a metaphor of the extraordinary impact of his father's demise and prophetic symbol of Agee's own self-destruction. Richard cradles the "bodiless shell" even as Rufus Agee held on to the memory of Jay Agee, preserved emblematically by the empty morris chair in *A Death in the Family*.

Death was alternately winsome and forbidding in the writer's mind. Like Richard, who thought about drowning as he held on to a rock at the bottom of the Sand Cut, Agee toyed with the idea of ending his life. Certainly he was preoccupied by death and depressed by it. Yet, as one propelled forward by thoughts not communicated and books not written, he found the idea of suddenly ending his life somehow too simple. He chose instead to "systematically destroy his beautiful body," in the words of Alma Neuman, engaging in a "deliberate, slow suicide." For Agee, existence needed to be complicated by living to excess: "talking passionately, brilliantly, but too much, drinking too much, smoking too much, reading aloud too much, making love too much." [60]

As a boy and as a man, James Agee never believed he was worthy to possess life, to enjoy ease and comfort. It was the husks, the bodiless shells, the crumbs under the table—cheap clothes, shabby apartments, and frayed nerves—that the writer, chastened by guilt, claimed as his due. So it is altogether appropriate that Agee closes *The Morning Watch* with Richard, like Hamlet contemplating Yorick's skull, clutching "in exquisite protectiveness" the locust husk "which rests against his heart."

60. Dwight Macdonald, "Jim Agee," in David Madden (ed.), *Remembering James Agee* (Baton Rouge: Louisiana State University, 1974), 138.

CHAPTER
FOUR

Home Again

And suddenly Eugene was back in space and color and in
time, the weather of his youth was round him, he was
home again.
Thomas Wolfe, *You Can't Go Home Again*

With the drafting of *The Morning Watch* in the spring of 1950, Jim
Agee moved a step closer to writing his novel. His interest in fictional
narrative dated, of course, from his Exeter days, but his enthusiasm
for autobiographical fiction had its origins in his "Knoxville: Summer, 1915," published by *Partisan Review* in 1938. This early piece
provided the kernel for an in-depth study of his boyhood, and in 1948
Agee began to work in earnest on what was to evolve into *A Death in
the Family*. This novel, on which the writer worked until his death,
explores in a different way the same quest theme that is fundamental
to *The Morning Watch*: "Agee was still searching for himself, but now
within his own family." [1]

In the opinion of his editor, David McDowell, *A Death in the Family* is Agee's masterpiece. This view is widely shared by such writer-
critics as John Updike, who believes that Agee's literary reputation
was assured with the novel's posthumous publication in 1957. Robert
Fitzgerald expresses it for many: "*A Death in the Family* . . . held so

1. W. M. Frohock, "James Agee: The Question of Unkept Promise," *Southwest Review*, XLII (Summer, 1957), 228.

steadily and clearly . . . Jim's power of realization, a contained power, fully comparable to that in the early work of Joyce." Cautioning readers to "let the easy remark die on your lips," Fitzgerald adds, "if it took him twenty years longer than it took Joyce, who else arrived at all?" Dwight Macdonald provides a noteworthy dissent from prevailing critical opinion, however. Although he believes that *A Death in the Family* is a competent novel, he also feels that it is rather typical of its "type." Agee, he affirms, will be best remembered for the unique, virtuoso passages of *Let Us Now Praise Famous Men.*[2]

Of the novel's intent, Agee wrote that "this book is chiefly a remembrance of my childhood and memorial to my father."[3] He was more specific, if superstitious, about the fictional narrative in a letter to Father Flye: "I think I'd better not talk much about the piece of writing. A novel . . . about my first 6 years, ending the day of my father's burial" ([March 2, 1948], *Letters*, 170–71). As in the case of *The Morning Watch*, the writer was pessimistic about his ability to remain balanced and in control of his task—even while experiencing a sense of promise: "On the whole, I feel hopeful about it, and I certainly need to feel hopeful. Underlying the hopefulness is utter lack of confidence, apathy, panic and despair. And I'd better not dwell on that just now, either, for I could much too easily slip into it" (*Letters*, 170–71).

Despite the novelist's familiar battle with ambivalence, this project represented the fulfillment of the long-standing ambition he had first expressed as a high school student. Agee also addressed himself to the work's *raison d'etre* in the "Dream Sequence," the unused surrealistic portion of *A Death in the Family*: "He should go back into those years. As far as he could remember; and everything he could remember; nothing he had learned or done since; nothing except (so well as he could remember) what his father had been as he had known

2. David McDowell, interview, December 30, 1976; John Updike, "No Use Talking," *New Republic*, August 13, 1962, p. 23; James Agee, *The Collected Short Prose of James Agee*, ed. Robert Fitzgerald (Boston: Houghton-Mifflin, 1962), 55; Dwight Macdonald, interview, December 30, 1976.

3. Agee, *Collected Short Prose*, 142–44.

himself, and what he had seen with his own eyes, and supposed with his own mind."[4] While it was impossible to divorce himself from his adult viewpoint, Agee's focusing of *A Death in the Family* on the character of six-year-old Rufus Follet allowed him to make use of what Andrew Lytle calls the "innocent eye." By adopting this fictional technique, the writer was able to filter adult perceptions through a child's awareness. Another critic has spoken of the opening of "Knoxville: Summer, 1915," "We are talking now of summer evenings in Knoxville, Tennessee in the time that I lived there so successfully disguised to myself as a child," as suggesting an "adult trapped in the body of a child."[5]

From this vantage point, then, James Agee commented on his childhood. The "Knoxville" section, posthumously added as a prologue to the novel by Agee's editor, David McDowell, evokes an image of wonder, joy, and deep family affection:

> On the rough wet grass of the back yard my father and mother have spread quilts. We all lie there, my mother, my father, my uncle, my aunt, and I too am lying there. First we were sitting up, then one of us lay down, and then we all lay down, on our stomachs, on our sides, or on our backs, and they have kept on talking. They are not talking much and the talk is quiet, of nothing in particular, of nothing at all. The stars are wide and alive, they seem each like a smile of great sweetness and they seem very near. (*ADF*, 7)

In a detailed seventeen-page plan for the novel, the writer pointed to the objective of the book's early portion: "Begin with com-

4. James Agee, "A Death in the Family" (autograph working draft, in Humanities Research Center, University of Texas at Austin). "Dream Sequence" is the title given this section of the manuscript by Victor Kramer, who theorizes that Agee intended it as an introduction. The pages are unnumbered.
5. Andrew Lytle, *A Death in the Family* panel discussion videotape transcription, October 13, 1972, in James Agee Memorial Library, St. Andrew's School; James Agee, *A Death in the Family* (New York: McDowell, Obolensky, 1957), 3, hereinafter cited in the text as *ADF* with page number; David Madden, *A Death in the Family* panel discussion, October 13, 1972.

plete security and simple pleasure and sensations." Leslie Fiedler has written of the nostalgic tone of *A Death in the Family* and Agee's need "to relive the child's sense of warm, safe involvement in love, to believe again that such security is immune from death and change." The writer's aunt, Paula Tyler, the Aunt Amelia of the novel, recalls those early days as being filled with intimate family gatherings.[6]

Even during the halcyon days leading up to Rufus' father's death, however, Agee shows the discord between the Follet parents. The first chapter of the novel begins with a disagreement between Rufus' mother and father. When Jay suggests to his son that they go to a Charlie Chaplin movie, Mary reacts with indignant prudishness: "Oh Jay! . . . That horrid little man!" With mock innocence Jay asks, "What's wrong with him?" The topic is a familiar one in the household, Agee tells us. In response to Mary's protests of "He's so *nasty*! . . . So *vulgar*!" Jay "laughed as he always did." The child's reaction to this tired charade is significant: "Rufus felt that it had become rather an empty joke" (*ADF*, 11).

The opening scene is a harbinger of the polarization operative in the Follets' marriage. The writer pictured Jay and Mary (and by extension, his own parents) as cultural opposites. According to Agee's notes for the novel, the principal characters were to be: "A middle-class religious mother. A father of country background. Two sets of relatives: hers, middle-class, northern-born, more or less cultivated; his, of the deep mountain country." The writer accentuated Jay's hill-born ways when, after the picture show, the father says to the son, "Well . . . reckin I'll hoist me a couple" (*ADF*, 15). At the bar, Jay Follet proudly tells the gathering, "That's my boy. . . . Six years old, and he can already read like I couldn't read when I was twict his age" (*ADF*, 16). The contrast between Jay's backwoods lineage and Mary's genteel upbringing becomes more prominent when Jay, awakened by a telephone call in the middle of the night, prepares to go to his ailing

6. James Agee, "A Death in the Family" (notes and manuscript, in Humanities Research Center, University of Texas at Austin); Leslie Fiedler, "Encounter with Death," *New Republic*, December 9, 1957, p. 25; Paula Tyler, telephone conversation, May 10, 1977.

father's bedside. When Mary reasons with him to wait until morning, Jay thinks to himself, "That's easy for *you* to say. He's not *your* father, and besides you've always looked down at him" (*ADF*, 28).

Apart from the educational, social, and cultural dissimilarities between the two, a potentially serious breach is revealed in their religious differences. After Jay has left the house Mary prays in her bed, confessing, "For there, Lord, as Thou knowest . . . is the true, widening gulf between us" (*ADF*, 53). As she contemplates the future and her continued devotion to the church, Mary visualizes increasing separation: "And it would widen, oh, inevitably because . . . they were going to be brought up, as Christian, Catholic children. . . . It was bound . . . in some important ways . . . to set his children apart from him, to set his own wife apart from him. (*ADF*, 54)

To Rufus Follet, his father "smelled like dry grass, leather and tobacco." The author employs manly, agrarian images to suggest Jay's character, but he also reveals that behind the child's respect for his father's mastery lay a measure of uneasiness and fear. Jay Follet sometimes communicated "a feeling that things might go wrong." The young boy "knew what that was because he overheard them arguing. Whiskey" (*ADF*, 101).

The sharpest and most clearly revealing interchanges between Rufus' parents occur in Agee's working drafts for the novel. In an eight-page manuscript, most of which was deleted from the book, the two frequently quarrel bitterly. Significantly, too, Agee uses the real names of both of his parents in the excised material. The difference in emotional tone between the variant manuscript and the book text is obvious. Early in the novel, for example, Mary tells Jay that her brother Andrew and Amelia, his wife, had to leave for home without saying goodbye, as they didn't want to disturb Jay while he was singing lullabies to Rufus. Showing some exasperation, Mary says to Jay, "You must have been in there nearly an hour!" (*ADF*, 95). In the variant manuscript, however, the reprimand is far sharper: "Jay you were in there *forever.*" The draft for the novel also includes a fragment of cool interchange not found in the published text. Mary, still

90

miffed by Jay's tardiness, speaks: "Well let's go to bed. It's high time. Do you want anything to eat?" When Jay answers in the negative, Mary brings the conversation to a firm close: "Well I'm going up then. Be sure and lock both doors." [7]

The crisp dialogue between Jay and Laura in the working draft of the novel is the prelude to a deeply probing interchange in the variant manuscript. As the couple lies awake in bed, Laura refers to an earlier argument:

> "Jay . . . I just can't stand always to be shut out like that. I'm just simply not going to stand for it. It isn't right."
> "Like what?"
> "You must know perfectly well what I mean. When I asked you what you were thinking about and you—just answered me in a way that absolutely shut me out in the cold. That's all."
> He lay silent remembering it and trying to figure out what to say.
> "Do you hear me Jay?"
> "Sure I hear you."
> "Well answer me then. For goodness sake *say* something."
> "Nothing to say."
> "What do you mean there's nothing. This is *serious* Jay." [8]

Despite the occasional tender, forgiving speeches in the variant manuscript, there is nothing in the novel that is so indicative of the "widening gulf" vividly portrayed in the first version. While we cannot know precisely Agee's impetus for excising the material or for ultimately choosing a fictional name for his mother in the novel, the conjecture that the writer found the characterization of Laura Agee Wright too harsh, too personally damning, is plausible. In commenting to his sister, Emma, about his use of the family in fiction,

7. Agee, "A Death in the Family" (autograph working draft).
8. *Ibid.*

91

Agee at one time said, "I would never want to do anything to hurt Mother or Father." Perhaps the novelist was comforting his sister with a half-truth. The scenes depicted in the unused portion, though fictionally rendered, do point to genuine marital tensions between husband and wife and the families from which they came. Joel and Emma Tyler originally opposed Laura's marriage to Jay Agee, and while Paula Tyler believes her sister and brother-in-law were "more intellectual" than her nephew described them, there were, unquestionably, pronounced social and cultural differences between the models for Agee's parent figures.[9]

In a note for the novel, Agee revealed his intention to show chiefly the relationship between Jay and Rufus. The book was to be "just the story of my relation with my father and, through that, as thorough as possible an image of him: winding into other things on the way but never dwelling on them."[10] The novelist's conception of the work changed, of course: the father is seen primarily as a figure in death rather than in life. Yet Agee never drifted from his original desire to make *A Death in the Family* a "memorial" to his father. In life and in death Jay Follet is the magnetic, centrally focused hero.

As the father and son walk home after the film, Jay "courteously" offers him a Life Saver, "man to man." The gesture, the author tells, "sealed their contract." For Rufus, it was proof of his father's confidence in him. The young boy remembers that Jay had asked him "only once" not to reveal a minor indiscretion to his mother. Now the father accepted the son as one worthy to share confidences: "Rufus had felt gratitude in this silent trust" (*ADF*, 16–17). On the way home, sucking on their Life Savers, they sit down in a vacant lot. The novelist intimates that the communion between father and son is sublime. Rufus senses that Jay is not anxious to go home and that his father is estranged from the world: "He felt that although his father loved their home and loved all of them, he was more lonely than the

9. Emma Agee Ling, telephone conversation, March 7, 1977; Paula Tyler, telephone conversation, May 10, 1977.
10. Agee, "A Death in the Family" (notes and manuscript).

contentment of family love could help" (*ADF*, 19). The child Rufus (like the adult writer) shares that sense of apartness symbiotically with his father. He recognizes his father's need to sit outside by himself at night, to listen to the leaves moving in the dark, and to spend a few minutes watching the stars. And yet, brimming with the pride of a man-child, Rufus knew his "own presence was fully as indispensable to this well-being" (*ADF*, 19).

Agee renders with exquisite tenderness the bond between the boy and his father. It is nowhere more lovingly evoked in the novel than in a later scene, where Rufus feels the darkness speaking to him. "You heard the man you call your father: how can you ever fear?" (*ADF*, 84). When his cries bring Jay, "the room opened full of gold," as Rufus' father stepped through the doorway. The metaphor ascribes mythical powers to the father. Jay becomes a light-bearer, a sun god, a Midas. Just as quickly, however, the young boy's father becomes fully human as he "gently" teases Rufus. The light banter rapidly subsides; Jay lifts the child's head and looks deeply into his eyes. A balance is achieved between the godlike creature who passes into the room—the essence of omnipotence—and the father who comforts his son: Rufus "felt the strength of the other hand, covering his chest, patting gently (*ADF*, 87). After lighting a series of matches to convince Rufus that the darkened corners of the room contain nothing forbidding, Jay sings a series of old and popular songs. During his rendition of "Sugar Babe" as he pats Rufus' forehead ("Go to sleep, honey. . . . Go to sleep now"), tears come into Jay's eyes as he thinks of his own boyhood home in the mountains and "his mother's face, her ridged hand mild on his forehead" (*ADF*, 94).

And so James Agee in his fictional creation of Jay Follet, a figure based closely on his own father, portrays him as warmly understanding, hearty, and jovial. Basic to Jay's personality, as Agee renders him, is his deep compassion and sensitivity: his leaving in the middle of the night for his father's bedside and his taking the time to make the bed to hold the warmth in for Mary. For the child-man Agee, Jay was the all-encompassing symbol of celebrative life, while Mary represented the refined, coolly repressive aspects of existence, the urge to contain that exuberance. "In this post-Victorian arcadia," Edwin Ruhe has observed, Rufus' father "stands unquestionably as an image of freedom, indulgence, joy in life, earthiness, and . . . loneliness." The elements of Jay's personality, as Ruhe assesses them, stand in decided contrast to Mary's "feminine-genteel impulse." Agee's female protagonist offers an archetype of wifely, motherly perfection. Jay's drinking inspires her censure; her strongly religious devotion produces intolerance; her urge toward respectability threatens to drive her husband and children from her side. Jay's hesitation to return home embodies his quiet yet firm resistance "to that representative heiress of Victorian authoritarianism, the much-loved, abundantly-loving, but not quite admirable Mary Follet." [11]

As with the autobiographical writing of *The Morning Watch*, much of *A Death in the Family* is faithful to the actual circumstances surrounding Jay Agee's death. Apart from the writer's use of his parents as models for his fictional characters, he incorporated the remainder of his immediate family as well. Father Flye felt that the characterization of Mary Follet's parents resembled Agee's Tyler grandparents very closely. But he agreed with Paula Tyler that the portrayal of Hugh Tyler as Uncle Andrew was much less faithful to the original. "That isn't exactly a good picture of him," Father Flye comments. "He was a gentler person than that and not so . . . caustic." Hugh Tyler, a professional muralist and amateur poet was "charming," warm, and endearing, according to the priest. [12]

In addition to basing virtually all the figures in the novel on family members, Agee anchored the plot line in authentic facts. When the Follets go to visit the great-great-grandmother (a fictional creation), the aged lady's companion, Aunt Sadie, tells Jay she mailed him a letter addressed to "Post Office, Cristobal, Canal Zone, Panama"; she didn't put a street address on the envelope, with "Jay working for the post office" (*ADF*, 236). The letter, sent long after Jay and

11. Edward Ruhe, Review of *A Death in the Family*, *Epoch*, VIII (Winter, 1958), 251.
12. James H. Flye, interview, December 28, 1976.

Mary had returned to Knoxville, was mailed to the exact location of Jay and Laura Agee's first home following their marriage, when Jay was a postal employee in Central America.

The call Jay Follet's brother, Ralph, made in the novel to come to his father's deathbed was also based on fact. Whereas the fictional Ralph is drunk and on the verge of panic when he telephones, however—"But O Lord, hit looks like the end, Jay!" (ADF, 25)—such was not the case when Frank Agee called his brother Jay. Annabel King Agee (Mrs. John Henry Agee) wrote, "Mossie (Hugh James' [Jay's] and John's sister) heard the conversation Frank had with Jim about the father's illness, and she told me there was nothing unusual about it—Frank was not drunk. So I will have to say that the book gives a very exaggerated description." [13]

Even though the writer embroidered the facts of the actual telephone call, he was, apparently, drawing closely from his memory of his uncle. Agee presents the fictive Ralph as an incompetent, maudlin undertaker, unable to cope with the prospect of his father's death. [14] His efforts to comfort his mother are pathetic and histrionic: "He came near her over and over again, hugging her, sobbing over her, fondling her, telling her that she must be brave, to lean on him, and cry her heart out. . . . Everyone in the room, even Ralph in the long run, knew he was only making things harder for her; only his mother realized he was beseeching comfort rather than bringing it" (ADF, 62).

In a sheaf of notes and fragments for the novel, the writer recorded his impressions of the morning of his father's funeral. He vividly described Frank's reaction in the east room of the family home: "Frank made a stumbling, sobbing rush for us and bellowed, heavily drunk with whiskey strong and sour on his breath, how it was all his fault, he'd never forgive himself, never; and who? Hugh? Frank's mother? Both? hurried to him saying, *control yourself,* and the mother

13. Annabel Agee to Walter B. Chambers, January 6, 1973, in James Agee Memorial Library, St. Andrew's School.
14. According to Paula Tyler, Frank Agee was also a mortician.

comforting him." [15] Agee did not choose to use the scene at Jay Follet's funeral, but he did weave portions of it into the fabric of the book. Just as Frank had tried to assume responsibility for Jay Agee's death, when Ralph is told that his brother is dead, he attempts to assuage his guilt by asking Andrew for the privilege of preparing the body. Andrew reports to his sister:

> "He's blaming himself for Jay's . . . . He wants to try to make up for it."
> "How on earth can he blame himself!"
> "For phoning Jay in the first place." (ADF, 182)

The novelist's presentation of his father's death—its cause and immediate aftermath—is almost entirely factually based. In speaking of Agee's fidelity to the sequence of events, Father Flye affirms that "the circumstances . . . were identical with those described in *A Death in the Family*." Hazel Lee Goff, Laura Agee Wright's close Knoxville friend, recalls May 18, 1916: "Certainly I remember the night of his death. . . . It was just like Rufus wrote in the book. A man from Ty-sa-man [a contraction of Tyler-Savage-Manning] Company where Jay worked came to the house shouting that Jay had been "hurt bad" in a wreck. Laura called her twin brother, Hugh Tyler (the artist), and he went to the scene and returned to tell her Jay was dead." [16] The only variation from the actual events in the fictional account is that the first witness to the accident in the novel telephones Mary, rather than coming in person, to tell her that her husband had been involved in a "serious accident" (ADF, 115).

Andrew's explanation for the car crash—that a cotter pin worked loose in the steering mechanism—is more complicated than Laura's theory about her husband's death. "Laura always felt," Miss Goff states, "and I do, too, that Jay fell asleep at the wheel. He had been working late the night before and had driven to the mountains to see

15. James Agee, "A Death in the Family" (notes and fragments of manuscript, in Humanities Research Center, University of Texas at Austin).
16. Quoted in Charles W. Mayo, "James Agee: His Literary Life and Work" (Ph.D. dissertation, George Peabody College, 1969), 8.

his ailing father that day. He never liked to stay away from his family all night so he started home after midnight and ran off the road before he could get there." [17]

Agee's description of the fatal accident is a wholly factual rendering of the actual tragedy. It was surmised that a rock hitting the car's front wheels wrenched the car violently, slamming Jay's chin against the steering wheel and instantly producing a fatal concussion. When Andrew tells Mary and the family the details of the accident, he notes that after the impact, the "auto threw him out on the ground as it careened down into the sort of flat, wide ditch, about five feet down from the road; then it went straight up on an eight-foot embankment" (ADF, 164). The fictional elucidation of the event is corroborated by Annabel King Agee, who said that she and her husband, John, were well aware that the elder Mr. Agee was seriously ill. When they received the telegram in Nebraska, Mrs. Agee assumed it was informing them of her father-in-law's death: "Such a shock when I read, 'Jim killed last night Car turned over embankment Father no better Love Frank.'" [18]

The writer also placed the scene of the accident at virtually the same spot. In A Death in the Family, when Mary telephones Andrew to ask him to go to Jay, she says that "a man just phoned, from Powell's Station, about twelve miles out" (ADF, 116–17). The John Henry Agees could not attend the funeral, so when they returned to Knoxville in September, 1916, they "went to see Laura and the children first thing." Of their conversation with her sister-in-law, Annabel Agee has written: "I remember her saying, 'And just to think Jay (as she called him) was within 12 miles of home.'" [19]

Another parallel between Agee's narrative and established fact is Mary's selection of "In his strength" for Jay's epitaph: "It's how he'd look Death itself in the face. It's how he did! . . . Those are the words that are going to be on his gravestone, Andrew" (ADF, 174). Louise

17. *Ibid.*
18. Annabel Agee to Walter B. Chambers, January 6, 1973, Agee Library.
19. *Ibid.*

Davis, a Knoxville writer and friend of Agee's mother confirmed that the inscription on Hugh James Agee's gravestone at the Greenwood Cemetery in Knoxville reads, "In His Strength." [20]

It is clear from both the factual and the fictional accounts of the fatal crash that the family felt compelled to find an explanation for Jay Agee's death. It cannot be conclusively determined, of course, whether a cotter pin worked loose (as Uncle Andrew explained it), or Jay fell asleep at the wheel (as Laura Agee believed), or even if drinking contributed to the accident. One senses that the Agee and Tyler families have a special antipathy to the implication of family drunkenness in *A Death in the Family*. They are quick to deny it, as in the case of Jay Agee's brother—"Frank was not drunk. . . . the book gives a very exaggerated description."

It is ironic that Laura Agee should have selected the pious epitaph, "In His Strength," for one so "sublimely indifferent" to organized religion. Mrs. Agee's seizing upon the phrase, in addition to the fictional family's almost wishful mythologizing about the death event, does give credence to the conjecture that they were terrified at the thought that Jay died drunk. Implicit in the epitaph is the belief that Jay's soul was not in peril, that he died in a state of grace, that he would join his Heavenly Father. Some of Agee's relatives, as the ones left to explain, are understandably sensitive about biographical and fictional parallels. James Agee's sister expressed a typical reaction: "It is, after all, only a novel." [21]

Because the ties between Agee's biography and his *oeuvre* are so numerous, however, we must consider the possibility that Agee was again drawing from life for Rufus Follet's observations about his father's fondness for liquor. While it has not been established that Jay Agee was an alcoholic, nevertheless, liquor figures prominently in the characterization of Jay Follett—particularly in his relationship with Mary. Agee tells us that Rufus "overheard them arguing. Whiskey."

20. Quoted in Mayo, "James Agee," 283.
21. Ling, telephone conversation, March 7, 1977.

The fact of crucial importance is not Jay's personality per se, but rather the effect of his attitudes upon his son. Alcoholism occurs in disproportionately large numbers among persons who have had alcoholic parents—a pattern owing largely to the conscious and subconscious modeling involved in any parent-child relationship. With Agee, who was desperate for his father's approval, who felt insecure about his own masculinity, and who idolized Jay Agee, it appears highly likely that the writer's emulation of his departed father-hero was always nearly certain.

Like Rufus Follet, Agee believed his father, with his rough clothes, heavy beard, and deeply tanned neck, was the prototypical male. The immaturity and weakness of young Rufus provide a contrast to the characteristics of Jay, the source "full of energy," the light-bearer: "His hands were so big he could cover him from the chin to his bath-thing. There were big blue strings under the skin on the backs of them. Veins, those were. Black hair even on the backs of the fingers and ever so much hair on the wrists; big veins in his arms, like ropes" (ADF, 101).

In addition to the young protagonist's worship of Jay's virility, of his childhood perception of masculinity, Rufus Follet-Agee may well have felt a psychic bond as well. The writer's strongly developed self-destructive instinct is also alluded to in Jay Follet's personality, as when he drives to his ailing father's bedside: "He felt thirsty, and images of stealthiness and deceit, of openness, anger and pride, immediately possessed him, and immediately he fought them off. If ever I get drunk again, he told himself proudly, I'll kill myself. And there are plenty of good reasons why I won't kill myself. So I won't even [sic] get drunk again" (ADF, 95). Most significantly, this Oedipal emphasis may have its logical, fitting conclusion in Agee's recurring fantasy that he would die at the age of thirty-six, as he wrote to the priest in 1945.[22]

For a variety of complex reasons, then, James Agee chose to act

22. James Agee, The Letters of James Agee to Father Flye (New York: George Braziller, 1962), 154.

99

out in his own life some of his father's characteristics. His life, like his fiction with its fidelity to actual circumstances, became a living memorial to the dear, departed past. It is highly meaningful that James Agee left the record virtually intact in describing Jay Follet's death and funeral. In his review of A Death in the Family, Edward Ruhe has commented perceptively about Andrew's awareness of "the sacred character" of the details surrounding Jay's demise.[23] The single tiny wound on Jay's chin, a fact combed over and repeated often by the characters in the novel, is obviously the most haunting, yet the most sacred piece of evidence to the family and to Agee himself. He explains the human phenomenon of needing to examine the death in minute detail when Mary has selected the words for Jay's grave marker. Her father, Joel, thinks to himself: "That's what they're there for, epitaphs. . . . So you can feel you've got some control over the death, you *own* it, you choose a name for it. The same with wanting to know all you can about how it happened. And trying to imagine it as Mary was" (*ADF*, 1974).

Indeed, the writer's need to master death and thereby cope with the shattering impact that the end of his father's life has upon him is at the heart of the novel. Alfred Kazin has suggested that Agee's "almost unbearable effort at objectivity" in the work sought "to externalize a private grief." So it is that the unreasonable, traumatizing fear of the dark that Rufus experiences becomes a metaphor for the blackness that will envelop the child-man mentally and emotionally. Jay Follet-Agee is the light-bearer—the dark room opens "full of gold" when he steps into it. He strikes matches to reveal the "truths" obscured in the shadowy corners. Understandably, then, Rufus Follet-Agee clings to his father, does not want him to leave or the darkness to cover him.[24] He is figuratively terrified of the light going out of his life and literally frozen by the prospect of losing his father in death.

23. Ruhe, Review of *A Death in the Family*, 250.
24. Alfred Kazin, "Good-By to James Agee," *Contemporaries* (Boston: Little, Brown, 1962), 187; Lytle, *A Death in the Family* panel discussion videotape transcription, October 13, 1972, in Agee Library.

It is because this loved object is suddenly taken from Rufus that a fierce anger is commingled with the child-man's grief. On the morning after his father is killed, the small boy feels a sense of anticipation "almost as if this were Christmas morning" (*ADF*, 249). As he proudly marches into his parents' bedroom wearing his new cap and calling "Daddy! Daddy!," Rufus is "brought up short in dismay, for his father was not there" (*ADF*, 249).

Rufus' reaction at not finding his father is psychologically in accord with the grief reaction discussed in chapter two, the common, feverish desire among orphaned children to find the lost, loved object. "Where's Daddy?" the young boy "shouted imperiously" to his mother. To her weak reply, "Daddy isn't here yet," Rufus "demanded in angry disappointment": "Where *is* he, then!" (*ADF*, 250). After Mary Follet explains to Rufus and Catherine, the fictional representation of Emma Agee, that their father has died, the children attempt to put the intelligence into their own graspable frame of mind. In an attempt to explain the event satisfactorily to themselves, Rufus and Catherine employ what Dr. William M. Lamers, Jr., a San Francisco psychiatrist, has called "magical thinking."[25] Through the child's use of a series of analogues, Dr. Lamers believes, a tangential understanding of death is achieved. Mary's explanation that "Daddy . . . got hurt and—so God let him go to sleep" (*ADF*, 251–52) is interpreted by Rufus to mean "he got hurt so bad God put him to sleep" (*ADF*, 258). The association which Catherine has with "put him to sleep" is translated (via magical thinking) to the following understanding: "Like the kitties, Catherine thought; she saw a dim, gigantic old man in white take her tiny father by the skin of the neck and put him in a huge slop jar of water and sit on the lid, and she heard the tiny scratching and the stifled mewing" (*ADF*, 258). Rufus, likewise, makes his own analogy: "Like the rabbits, Rufus remembered, all torn white bloody fur and red insides. He could not imagine his father like that" (*ADF*, 259).

25. William M. Lamers, Jr., "The Absent Father," in Edward V. Stein (ed.), *Fathering: Fact or Fable?* (Nashville: Abingdon, 1977), 70.

101

The violent, sadistic images called up in the minds of Rufus and Catherine—quite apart from the children's innocence—are rooted in deep anger. They are born of the desire to "get back" or "get even" with the offending party, Jay, to make him pay for the anguish and suffering brought upon them, the innocent victims. Such feelings of betrayal, of being "cheated" of a father, also take other forms, as when Rufus realizes: "He has been dead since way last night and I didn't even know until I woke up" (*ADF*, 263). Even less subtle and more demonstrative of Rufus' aggression is his telling the boys in the neighborhood "shyly and proudly" that "My daddy's dead" (*ADF*, 269).

That Rufus sensed "something deeply wrong" in smiling at the prospect of telling his friends about the death is, of course, his way of registering a guilt feeling. This frequent concomitant of the grief process becomes an important, unsettling influence in Rufus' psyche. He tortures himself with the repeated refrain "How would your daddy like it?" and tries to develop a standard by which to measure his integrity. Rufus chides himself for bragging about his new status as a child bereft of a father: "Showing off because he's dead, that's all you can show off about" (*ADF*, 280).

Then, in a passage of searing intensity, the elements within the grief mechanism become largely externalized. As the child-man Rufus regrets his "showing off," he experiences a torrent of displacement, anger, guilt, fear, love and sympathy:

> He felt so uneasy, deep inside his stomach, that he could not think about it any more. He wished he hadn't done it. He wished he could go back and not do anything of the kind. He wished his father could know about it and tell him that yet he was bad but it was all right he didn't mean to be bad. He was glad his father didn't know because if his father knew he would think even worse of him than ever. But if his father's soul was around, always, watching over them, then he knew. And that was worst of anything because there was no way to hide from a soul, and no way to talk to it, either. He just knows, and it couldn't

102

say anything to him, and he couldn't say anything to it. It couldn't whip him either, but it could sit and look at him and be ashamed of him.

"I didn't mean it," he said aloud. "I didn't mean to be bad."

I wanted to show you my cap, he added, silently.

He looked at his father's morsechair.

Not a mark on his body.

He still looked at the chair. With a sense of deep stealth and secrecy he finally went over and stood beside it. After a few moments, and after listening most intently, to be sure that nobody was near, he smelled of the chair, its deeply hollowed seat, the arms, the back. There was only a cold smell of tobacco and, high along the back, a faint smell of hair. He thought of the ash tray on its weighted strap on the arm; it was empty. He ran his finger inside it; there was only a dim smudge of ash. There was nothing like enough to keep in his pocket or wrap up in a paper. He looked at his finger for a moment and licked it; his tongue tasted of darkness. (*ADF*, 280–81)

This section of the novel is somewhat muted, however; Rufus' original fury has been transposed to the poignant awareness that there is nothing tangible by which to remember his father: "There was nothing like enough to keep in his pocket or wrap up in a paper." The deepest point of the child's rage has been absorbed mentally and emotionally. In Agee's notes for the novel he summarized the telling effect of the father's death: "The child is in a sense and degree doomed, to religion and to the middle class. The mother: to religiosity. New strains develop."[26]

Agee's childhood attitude toward religion and authority can be seen in his portrayal of Father Jackson in *A Death in the Family*. The figure of the officiating priest at Jay Follet's rites was based on Father Robertson, a clergyman who "came specially from Chattanooga." Agee pictured Father Jackson as a pompous prig, but according to Father Flye, "I asked James' mother about that detail and she said he

26. Agee, "A Death in the Family" (notes and manuscript).

103

was not that way at all." Obviously, though, the writer's perceptions at six years old were widely different from his mother's. In his notes on his father's funeral, Agee wrote with feeling about what he perceived as Father Robertson's attempt to take Jay's place: "I realized faintly that he was the boss of this occasion, and obscurely resented his bossiness and intrusion, his sureness of his right to be there."[27] Agee's injured sensibilities are displayed in the novel: "Father Jackson strode efficiently across the room sat in their father's chair, crossed his knees narrowly, and looked, frowning, at the carefully polished toe of his right shoe. They watched him, and Rufus wondered whether to tell him whose chair it was" (ADF, 291).

The boy Agee's bitter, sharply felt pain at the priest's "intrusion" is indicative of deep insecurity. The little boy found himself on an unlighted, uncertain path after Jay's death—"his tongue tasted of darkness." This line, the product of the adult Agee's years of deep brooding, depression, and insecurity, is closely related to a passage in the "Dream Sequence," where a strikingly similar chorus of anger and grief echoes within Rufus when he awakes from the dream: "He thought of all he could remember about his father and about his own direct relations with him. He could see nothing which even faintly illuminated his darkness." And then Agee adds, in a phrase brimming with the sad wisdom of adulthood, "nor did he expect ever to see anything."[28]

In A Death in the Family, Rufus earnestly wishes to show his father "man to man" the new cap, which he buys, significantly, on the morning of Jay's death, because it is an emblem of his growth from child to boy. When she takes him out to buy the cap, Rufus' Aunt Hannah, to her credit Rufus thinks, bypasses Miller's, "a profoundly matronly store" where Mary had always purchased her son's clothes, and opts for Harbison's, "clothing exclusively for men and boys." Among Rufus' contemporaries, the latter establishment is regarded

27. Flye, interview, December 28, 1976; Agee, "A Death in the Family" (notes and fragments of manuscript).
28. Agee, "A Death in the Family (autograph working draft).

as " 'tough' and 'sporty' and 'vulgar' " (*ADF*, 77). The boy's decision
to buy the ill-fitting, "thunderous fleecy check in jade green, canary
yellow, black and white" cap, complete with monstrous visor, is
motivated by considerably more than a desire to be *au courant*. In
Agee's notes for the novel, he provides a fuller explanation for the
purchase of the hat: "He is drawn always more deeply into his
mother's orbit, always the more wishing he could be in his father's.
Every opportunity to do what he thinks his father would approve,
meant much to him. A cap is just an example. . . . The child . . . is
sure this will make him more masculine and that his father will be
pleased."[29]

Not surprisingly, then, Rufus believes the presentation of the cap
to be an august and profound occasion ("almost . . . Christmas
morning"). The child's intense desire for his father's approval, and the
cap as the means to achieve it, follow from a marginal note that Agee
made in his plan for the novel: "From the moment he had it [the cap]
he could think of only one thing: to show it to his father."[30]

The story of the cap is also revealing because the boy Rufus views
himself as caught between his parents and not totally acceptable to
either. Agee described the Rufus persona as "a soft and somewhat precocious child," whose "deficiency . . . puts them [Jay and Mary] at
odds." It is known that as a child Agee studied painting in his Uncle
Hugh's studio and learned piano from his Aunt Paula.[31] Quite possibly, he felt uneasy about participating in these refined, artistic pas-
times, in view of his father's unfamiliarity with them.

More specifically, the writer's notes seem to suggest that a Knoxville neighbor, Mr. Tripp, and his father attempted at one point to
teach him to fight—an exercise that ended badly. Speaking of himself
in an autobiographical fragment, the writer recalled the incident in
the third person: "He doesn't understand why he should fight, and he

29. Agee, "A Death in the Family" (notes and fragments of manuscript).
30. *Ibid.*
31. Jeanne M. Concannon, "The Poetry and Fiction of James Agee: A Critical Analysis," (Ph.D. dissertation, University of Minnesota, 1968), 4.

is too trusting." Jay's "efforts to show him how" to fight, Agee's notes continue, "complete making a coward of him and make him need the father's approval." Laura, according to the novelist, fearful that her son was being mistreated, "over-defends him," which "further puts the father off."[32]

It is notable that the author, throughout the notes for the work and in *A Death in the Family* itself repeatedly sounds the theme of personal failure and his need for his father's approbation. The beginning of his plan for the novel is illustrative: "Theme: I worship him: I fail him: I need his approval: he is killed: everything is changed. (2nd theme: he is at an uneasy time of his life. My failure hurts him)." Among the novel's elements, Agee listed as the first, "the father and son relationship—admiration—need for respect—fear." Later, in his scheme for the work the writer made this notation: "Keep father-son undertone, uncertainty of his esteem."[33]

Nowhere is the theme of yearning for his father's favor within the grief cycle more forthrightly laid out than in the "Dream Sequence."[34] In this haunting, disturbing dream, the boy Rufus, though never called by name, who has grown to manhood, realizes that he is in downtown Knoxville. The adult persona, like the boy, is obviously the Agee stand-in, for he rounds a corner with "the loose stride inherited from the mountains." As he walks, the man sees ahead a crowd of people "doing some terrible piece of violence." His impulse is to pause. "The pit of his stomach went cold, yet now he felt really at home." In addition to revealing some sadistic impulses, the Rufus figure expresses a kind of death wish, acting out a semi-delusional expectation of punishment by thinking that the crowd might "turn on me, that's all right to[o]. Not just exactly, but the way it was meant to be. . . . it was not his business to try to alter fate." This curiously deterministic view of the universe and the man's own involvement in it is characteristic of Agee's passivity and ten-

32. Agee, A Death in the Family (notes and manuscript).
33. *Ibid.*
34. Agee, "A Death in the Family" (autograph working draft).

dency toward masochism. Moreover, the fatalism in the "Dream Sequence" may also be found in a long passage in the working draft for the novel, which was excised. Laura says, "I don't know when. Or which of us. Maybe all of us. But something dreadful is going to happen, Jay: Something irreparable. To our family, somehow in that auto."[35] Although this particular passage did not find its way into the novel, Agee's thematic emphasis on determinism is pervasive in *A Death in the Family*, particularly in the description of Jay's accident and his wound. Apart from the mystique surrounding the tiny cut on his chin, Andrew tells Mary that the car came to rest "right beside" her husband, "without even grazing him!" (*ADF*, 164). The fated sense of the crash is given additional prominence when Andrew reports on his conversation with the doctor: "He says it was just a chance in a million. . . . Just that one tiny area, at just a certain angle, and just a certain sharpness of impact. If it had been even a half an inch to one side, he'd be alive this minute" (*ADF*, 165).

As the "Dream Sequence" continues, the Agee stand-in comes closer and the crowd disperses, revealing the corpse of a man whom they have murdered. The protagonist recognizes the man as John the Baptist. He thinks of John as "the old loudmouth . . . the old ranter" and does so "with affection." The sight of the dead man (who was from "way back in the country") fills the Rufus figure with compassion: "His heart spread and he loved the *brave* old bellower misled and misleading." The writer's use of pejorative terms to describe John the Baptist ("old loudmouth" and "old ranter") and his statement that he thinks of the man "with affection," sets up a characteristic Agee duality. It may well be a comment on his own ambivalent responses to the Church, but is more likely made in response to his dead father. As the "Sequence" continues, elements of Jay Agee's personality become more obvious in the portrayal of John the Baptist and, finally, dominate the Baptist figure entirely. The allusion to the father's hill-born roots in this passage ("way back in the country") is unmistakable. In

35. *Ibid.*

addition, Agee's use of the term *brave*—underlined in his manuscript—to describe the man is significant, for it echoes the "Dedication" poem of *Permit Me Voyage*, where Agee speaks of "my brave father." The writer could certainly have thought his father to be a
"bellower" for his hearty, jovial enthusiasm. That the man is also
called "misled and misleading" may have reference to Agee's feeling
about his father's country background, that he believed Jay had no
real opportunity to succeed in life or to equip his mind, and that the
Tylers never understood or appreciated his mountain ways and lineage. Finally, the merging of the John the Baptist figure and Jay Agee
into a single persona, whether subconsciously through an actual
dream or consciously in his fictional creation, is consistent with
Agee's intent to make the novel a memorial to his father. John the
Baptist, who lived a rude, simple existence "way back in the country"
and who was a saintly personage, would have easily met Agee's re-
quirement for a historical model suitable for the writer's own
"canonization."

The Agee persona in the "Dream Sequence" feels the need to treat
the body kindly, to let it "lie out in the open, but in honor and in
state." He stoops down, cradles the body "like a baby" and begins to
carry the corpse. As the man walks with his burden, he realizes it has
been "so many years" since he had been in Knoxville, yet he remembers the way. He makes for "a certain corner, a vacant lot; he could
already see it vividly in his mind's eye." Ironically, and significantly,
that place is the destination of Rufus and his father in *A Death in the
Family* after viewing the Chaplin movie and going to the bar: "It was a
vacant lot, part rubbed bare clay, part over-grown with weeds, rising
a little from the sidewalk" (*ADF*, 17).

During the journey through Knoxville, the man is painfully conscious of the stares of the townspeople: "He could feel their eyes
on him after he had passed. . . . he knew the eyes were still on
him. . . . he could feel their eyes again." The emphasis on being
watched and the resentment that the bystanders produce in the persona is reminiscent of Agee's notes about his father's funeral. When

Laura Agee, Emma, and Rufus were brought in to view the body, the writer remembered the mourners' eyes upon the family: "I was most appalled by and interested in the feeling that everybody was looking at us." [36]

In his progress toward the vacant lot, the man feels guilty about his inability to carry the body properly: "He was filled with shame. He found the body had sagged clumsily during his carelessness, and he readjusted his hold, to carry it more decently." This statement relates importantly to Agee's objective in the novel to develop the plot around the boy's seeking after the father's affirmation of him and the boy's feeling "deficient" about holding his love. It is psychologically meaningful that, as the protagonist comes to "their corner . . . the vacant lot," the spot which expressed Rufus' father's nature, the psychic burden, the body, becomes too heavy and has to be put down.

The close link between the mental perception and physical fact accentuates the ambivalent feelings that the man has about the remains. The corpse has been steadily decomposing in the heat, giving off an overpowering stench. The Rufus figure cannot bring himself to carry the stinking body any longer, as it is now "streaked with brown." Later, when snow suddenly appears on the ground, "blue streaks as big as the brown," evidence of the freezing weather, help to preserve the body. The head, however, fares much worse, becoming "a kind of transparent gristle, yellowish and rubbery." Agee's macabre portrayal of the disintegration of John's body becomes an aggressive, hostile parody of his father's virtually unscathed corpse.

John the Baptist, who certainly is something of a father figure, is also figuratively a child, cradled in the man's arms. When the smell finally overpowers him, the Rufus figure "began to slowly drag the body along the pavement like a sled." A by-product of the dragging is the guilt feeling it promotes: "Again he wondered whether he could possibly carry him. . . . It's a hell of a way to treat anyone, but it'll have to do." When the man is cognizant that like John, he too is

---

36. Agee, "A Death in the Family" (notes and fragments of manuscript).

naked, and that his feet are bleeding and frozen, he experiences "a sense of courage, difficulty, and dignity, so that he felt gravely cheerful, and knew there was a smile on his face." This passage points back not only to Rufus' sublime joy in announcing his father's death—proclaiming his victory over Jay, living while he has died—but also to Richard's fantasies of self-mortification in *The Morning Watch* and Agee's qualified masochism in *Let Us Now Praise Famous Men*.

As the man and the corpse reach the vacant lot, a parallel description of Rufus' and Jay's rendezvous site "twenty years later," is seen. In *A Death in the Family* Agee writes, "There was a medium-sized tree and near enough to be within its shade in daytime, an outcrop of limestone like a great bundle of dirty laundry" (*ADF*, 18). In the "Dream Sequence" he returns to the spot: "And sure enough he could see it, with a flinching deep within him of tenderness and joy and melancholy and great loneliness, he could see it, the very corner, the same outcrop of wrinkled limestone, like a lump of dirty laundry, the same tree even, and the tree had not even grown an inch. So shabby and sad; it had been waiting there all this time, and it had never changed, not a bit."

The tree is a personification of Rufus' own mixed feelings—of loyalty to his father, "waiting there all this time . . . never changed, not a bit," and anger at his suddenly leaving him ("So patient, and aloofly welcoming. Well. So you came back.") This epiphany, this *déjà vu* is short-lived. The Rufus figure absent-mindedly jerks the body over "the curb just opposite its corner," and the shreds holding the head to the trunk are severed, sending the head rolling into the street. The head turns in upon itself "like a jellyfish, an armadillo," and then finally, "like a Grail." As it decomposes into an indistinguishable mass, the child-man wakes up.

A plausible interpretation of the rotting, decaying corpse is the link between it, Jay Agee's death, and the boy Agee's ensuing anger and terror. The dead father's dreams and ambitions for his son weigh on the Rufus figure like a millstone. He can't free himself of the responsibility to be the dutiful, promising son—to "make up" for the

110

life his father could not live. The Rufus figure attempts to become a father to his own father, cradling the corpse in his arms, but cannot physically or emotionally bear the awesome responsibility. It is when the Rufus figure drags the body like a sled that it begins to decompose. Agee follows the romantic tradition in the "Dream Sequence" by idealizing the natural world. Reality forces him to understand his father in death as a naked, unlovely corpse. The knowledge fills the Agee persona with guilt and shame, and he chastizes himself during the journey, "It's a hell of a way to treat anyone."

This series of ambivalent responses—alternately loving and hating the corpse—particularly comes into play just before the Rufus figure awakens. When the man's head rolls down the street, it is radically different from the head of John the Baptist, ceremoniously displayed on a platter. This head is a mockery, a fraud, a ludicrous representation of a head. It is not even the embodiment of the Christian symbol of the fish, but a pretended emblem, "a jellyfish." That it does become "like a Grail" is true to Agee's characteristic pattern of advance and retreat—his pious and profane responses—to the world around him. Interestingly, "the Grail," too, is counterfeit: the dreamer is denied truth—as Agee was prevented from learning his own life's riddle by Jay's sudden death—when the "Chalice" quickly decomposes.

The Rufus figure, who helplessly watches the beheading of John with "sickness and grief" and "pity and shame," tries to put the dream into perspective. He is consumed by guilt: "The head had come off just short of the corner, and it was he who was responsible. The corner was where he used to sit with his father and it was here of all times and places that he had known best that his father loved him." The responsibility which the Agee stand-in feels has an interesting analogue to the writer's notations about his cowardice in being unable to fight. His failure to defend himself against Mr. Tripp and his father at the same corner makes it a place deeply divided in his mind, a source of pride and shame. As Agee stated in his plan for *A Death in the Family*, "I do badly at the corner." As the images of John

111

the Baptist and his father merge, the man in the "Dream Sequence" concludes, "I've betrayed my father. . . . Or myself. Or both of us." Despite his shame, hostility is still focused toward the man's father, caricatured earlier as a wild, saintly mountain man: "Even if they could talk, they could never come at it between them, what the betrayal was."

And then as the Rufus figure whispers the words, "My father," he feels "for a few moments it was as if his father were there in the room." There is a similar occurrence in *A Death in the Family* when the family, just after learning of Jay's death, senses his spirit among them: "It began to seem to Mary, as to Hannah, that there was someone in the house other than themselves. . . . 'It's Jay,' Mary whispered" (*ADF*, 185). The mystical incident, like so many in the novel, actually happened, according to Father Flye. The priest asked Hugh Tyler (not a "credulous person," in Father Flye's estimation) about it, and he said that somehow they "did feel his presence in the room."[37]

The visage that the man in the "Dream Sequence" sees in his mind's eye is the man for whom he has looked, "James Agee, my brave father," as he wrote in "Dedication." But the father has aged since he was a little boy, and is now "a strong, brave, sad old man who also knew the dream." The afterlife appearance of Jay Follet-Agee in life, in dream, and in fiction advances the theory proposed by Jeanne M. Concannon, that instead of an introduction to *A Death in the Family*, the "Dream Sequence" "may have been intended to extend the butterfly image of the resurrection which Rufus and Andrew share in the final chapter of the book."[38]

The story of Andrew telling Rufus about the butterfly is faithful to Agee's own recollection of Uncle Hugh's description of the graveside service. The illustration in the novel is close to the original of Agee's memory:

37. Flye, interview, December 28, 1976.
38. Concannon, "The Poetry and Fiction of James Agee," 125.

"If anything ever makes me believe in God," his uncle said, ". . . Or life after death. . . . It'll be what happened this afternoon.

"Right when they began to lower your father into the ground, into his grave, a cloud came over and there was a shadow just like iron, and a perfectly magnificent butterfly settled on the—coffin, just rested there.

"He stayed there all the way down . . . until it grated against the bottom. . . . And just when it did the sun came out just dazzling bright and he flew up out of that— hole in the ground."

Miraculous. Magnificent. He was sure he had better not ask what they were. . . . he felt that he probably had a fair idea of what "magnificent" meant. (*ADF*, 334–35)

The resemblance to the actual incident is apparent in Agee's notes on Hugh Tyler's description:

But mainly I remember his [Hugh's] needing to tell me about the butterfly. "If ever I believe in God, it will be because I remember what I saw today. The—coffin, with your father in it, was just being lowered and was just level with the ground, when a perfectly magnificent butterfly alighted on it, and just stood there for several seconds while they kept on lowering the coffin, the fools, and then a short cloud came off the sun and that had made every-thing dark, and just drowned everything in brightness, and it flew up straight to the sun." I don't know what mag-nificent means but through the word and the way he says it I am filled with a mysterious sense of glory.[39]

The writer's use of the butterfly, the Christian symbol of immor-tality, combines with the "visit" he has with his father after the dream. In his anger and grief, the Rufus figure thinks: "All his life, as he had begun during recent years to realize, had been shaped above all else by his father and by his father's absence." The Agee stand-in speaks for the novelist directly as he remembers the aftereffects of his

39. Agee, "A Death in the Family" (notes and fragments of manuscript).

father's death: "All his life he had fiercely loathed authority and had as fiercely loved courage and mastery." And then the writer appears to comment upon the host of formative male influences in his life—Joel Tyler, Father Flye, Professor Saunders, and Hugh Tyler, chief among them, "In every older man, constantly, he had looked for a father, or fought him, or both."

Because of the deeply psychological nature of the "Dream Sequence," one must be sensitive to the variety of factors that affected its production. Mia Agee recalls that during the 1940s she gave Jim a Rorschach test as a birthday gift. He was fascinated by it and spent twelve hours interpreting what he saw to the Jungian analyst, Frances Gillespy Wickes, the author of *The Inner World of Childhood*, which had so absorbed Agee at Anna Maria Key. Agee decided to go into therapy. The writer had been intrigued by dream analysis since reading Mrs. Wickes's book, and her pronouncement that Agee's reading of the Rorschach was "fantastic" appears to have lessened his fear of therapy. This type of mental exploration was far less threatening to him than Freudian psychoanalysis. Agee admired Freud intellectually, Mia Agee affirms, but "always knew that wasn't for him." [40] "I would somewhere near as soon die (or enter a narcotic ward)," the novelist wrote to Father Flye in the fall of 1941, "as undergo full psychoanalysis, I don't trust anyone on earth that much; and I see in every psychoanalyzed face a look of deep spiritual humiliation or defeat. . . . The look of "I am a man who finally could not call his soul his own but yielded it to another" (September 21, 1941, *Letters*, 127).

Jungian analysis seemed to be fairly palatable to the writer by the mid to late 1940s. As the later letters indicated, Agee took a more pragmatic, solicitous stance toward his own well-being at the end of the decade. In agreeing to undergo Jungian analysis, he acted on the desire he mentioned in the letter to Father Flye: "There is much I might learn and be freed from that causes me and others great pain, frustration and defeat, and I expect that sooner or later I will have to

40. Mia Agee, interview, March 24, 1977.

seek their help" (*Letters*, 127). The writer and Mrs. Wickes, according to Mia Agee, had a relaxed patient-therapist relationship because they "both liked each other very much."[41] James Agee was involved in Jungian therapy "for a year or two" in the period around 1948, the date generally accepted as the real genesis of *A Death in the Family*. Further confirmation of a similar time frame for the novelist's involvement in analysis and the composition of the "Dream Sequence" is given by the Rufus figure, who places the date as "towards the middle of the twentieth century."

While it is not known whether the "Dream Sequence" was based on an actual dream of Agee's, it appears likely. In the sequence itself, the authorial persona thinks that "he had dreamed the dream, for its own sake, without attempting to interpret." Yet the writer's long plan for the novel, which is replete with questions to ask friends and family members, includes this cryptic entry: "Dream: If you know what this means, or whether it means anything, I wish you would tell me." Dr. Robert Coles, the Harvard psychiatrist and protégé of Erik Erikson, confessed to being "utterly intrigued" by the "Sequence," finding it to be remarkably singular—"so vivid, so dramatic, so haunting." "It feels like a dream," Mia Agee states. "I would suspect it is an actual dream Jim had, but that is only conjecture."[42] It is not hard to understand why, if Agee did, in fact, dream this particular dream, he felt the need to write it down.

Certainly, *A Death in the Family*, the "Dream Sequence," and the writer's notes, stand as passionate, eloquent testaments to the crucible that a father's death was for a son. In his assessment of the novel, Dr. Coles has written: "The death in his family was more than a trauma, more than an awful moment. . . . Rufus is marked by the event." Yet through the searing pain of losing a man he loved, the psychiatrist suggests, Rufus Agee received a special understanding, a heightened awareness of manners, pretenses, and sensibilities within

41. Mia Agee, telephone conversation, May 19, 1977.
42. Agee, "A Death in the Family" (notes and manuscript); Robert Coles to the author, April 8, 1977; Mia Agee, telephone conversation, May 19, 1977.

his own family. All that rich lode, of course, was to be mined by James Agee throughout his life in fiction: "Rufus one day did redeem Jay and Mary Follett." [43]

James Agee, a man who wore the mantle of an artist, always sought, despite his disclaimer, to interpret. That he should choose in his last novel to depict actual events and portray his own family members most often literally, sometimes with modification, and rarely with pure invention, is telling. In his striking, detailed attention to fact, the novelist wanted to plumb the depths of a bitter, haunting mystery, to feel, as his fictional grandfather suggested, that he had "some control over the death," that he owned it, that he had chosen a name for it. For the writer, the novel was an extended opportunity to come to terms with his troubling past, his anger, shame, grief, and love. "Meeting" Jay Agee again in the "Dream Sequence" may well have been the approving, affirming experience he so longed for. "Thank you for coming," the Agee stand-in says to the departing figure. "Goodbye, God keep you." The "Sequence" protagonist reasons that, most probably, his father "would never return," but he decides "that was all right."

Out of the blackness that surrounded the child Rufus Follett emerged the man James Agee, "not the one who might have been, had Jay Follett lived a full life," and not one who was a "mere survivor," [44] but the one who thinks at the conclusion of the "Dream Sequence," "His father did not say goodbye but he knew of his brief smile, much as it always had been, and then he was gone. He was alone again now, but that was no harm, for in a way in which he had been alone for so many years, he knew he would never be alone again." The little boy, who watched his father strike matches to brighten darkened corners, grew up with lights of his own to open shadowy fictional rooms "full of gold."

43. Robert Coles, "Childhood: James Agee's A Death in the Family," Irony in the Mind's Life (Charlottesville: University Press of Virginia, 1973), 105.
44. Ibid., 106.

CHAPTER
FIVE

Empty Grail

Something troubled him which he had done or had left un-
done, some failure of the soul or default of the heart which
he could not now quite remember or perhaps forsee; he was
empty and idle, in some way he had failed. Yet he was also
filled to overflowing with a reverent and marveling peace
and thankfulness. My cup runneth over, something whispered within him, yet what he saw in his mind's eye was a
dry chalice, an empty Grail.

James Agee, *The Morning Watch*

James Agee left his job at *Time* in late 1948 to write a series of *Life*
essays on the film industry. Agee wrote two: a study of silent film
comedians, "Comedy's Greatest Era," published in September, 1949,
and "Undirectable Director," a piece about John Huston, printed in
September, 1950. With characteristically painstaking effort, it took
him six months to do the two assignments.[1]

Agee soon found the salary *Life* paid him too modest to live on.
He secured a contract to write film scripts based on two Stephen
Crane short stories, "The Blue Hotel" and "The Bride Comes to
Yellow Sky." Agee found the prospect of working in film thrilling.
The trip to the movie theater that Jay and Rufus make in *A Death in
the Family* points to one of Agee's greatest pleasures. The novelist and
his sister, Emma, as older children, frequently saw up to four films in

---

1. Tom Dardis, *Some Time in the Sun* (New York: Scribner's, 1976), 208.

four different theaters in a single Saturday. Agee's passion for the medium continued at Exeter and Harvard and reached consummation in his *Time* film reviews. "He loved movies more than anyone I ever knew," Robert Fitzgerald has written of his friend. "He also lived them and thought them." For Fitzgerald, "To see and hear him describe a movie that he liked—shot by shot, almost frame by frame—was unquestionably better in many cases than to see the movie itself."[2]

After completing the two film scripts written under contract to Huntington Hartford, and writing the commentary for his friend Helen Levitt's film, *The Quiet One*, Agee received an invitation to work with John Huston. The writer found the prospect of writing a screenplay for the director enormously attractive. "By 1950 John Huston was the favorite 'young' American director [then forty-four] . . . for those who took their films as seriously as Agee did." Huston had at that time a considerable personal and professional reputation. He began as a professional boxer while still in his teens, spent two years in the Mexican cavalry, wrote a book by the age of twenty-four (*Frankie and Johnny*), edited magazines, and finally worked as a writer at Warner Brothers. *Jezebel, Juarez, High Sierra*, and *Sergeant York* were among his screenwriting credits. It was John Huston's masterful directing of *The Maltese Falcon*, however, which established him as something more than a superb scriptwriter. The combination of Huston's talents was a strong inducement to the novelist: "It was Huston's huge success as a writer/director that most attracted Agee to work for him."[3]

Following the birth of his second daughter, Andrea Maria, in May of 1950 and the completion of *The Morning Watch* that spring, the writer set out for Hollywood in the fall. Agee's assignment was to write the article on Huston and a film script for *The African Queen*, based on the novel by C. S. Forester. Huston and Agee got on well

2. *Ibid.*, 196; Robert Fitzgerald, "A Memoir," in *The Collected Short Prose of James Agee*, ed. Robert Fitzgerald (Boston: Houghton-Mifflin, 1962), 49–50.
3. Dardis, *Some Time in the Sun*, 211, 212.

together—each attracted by the larger-than-life gestures of the other. The director was impressed by Agee's lack of pretense: his "dark and shiny" clothes, scuffed shoes, and rumpled shirts. "I doubt whether he had any idea of what he looked like," Huston has written. "Vanity wasn't in him." Even to the boisterous, unpredictable Huston, Agee was immoderate. Apart from his chain-smoking and the fact he was "a bottle-a-night man," the director recalled other evidence of Agee's self-destructiveness: "He held his body in very slight regard altogether." He ate "whatever was at hand," slept "when there was nothing else to do," and was "begrudging" about taking medicine.[4]

Agee and Huston also played highly competitive, powerful games of tennis. The combination of frenetic activity and an exhausting work schedule helped to bring on James Agee's first heart attack in January, 1951. In a letter written from Cottage Hospital, Santa Barbara, later in the month, the novelist spoke about his "modest edition of a coronary thrombosis" to Walker Evans. He complained of his illness with black humor: "The least one can do is drop dead, and apparently that is fairly often done. However, I got off light." It is clear that the attack again raised frightening questions within Agee about his mortality: "Quite a blow at 41, but so far, outside of occasional depressed moments, I don't much mind. I guess I'm still feeling too lucky at being alive and at not being turned into a permanent invalid."[5]

As he had before the appendectomy a year earlier, Agee felt in peril of his soul and turned confessionally to Evans. After indicating that Mia was arriving from Los Angeles that evening and would be with him the next day, he wrote:

> Christ how I wish I could pray, and mean, "From all adulterous liaisons, and deceptions of the trustful, and divi-

4. John Huston, Foreword to *Agee on Film, Volume II: Five Film Scripts* (New York: McDowell, Obolensky, 1960), ix.
5. James Agee to Walker Evans [January 22, 1951(?)] in Humanities Research Center, University of Texas at Austin.

119

sions of the heart, good Lord, Deliver us." I couldn't. But how lousy it is. It's bad enough when as seems to be usual only one woman is loved. But this I really hate, and of course an [?] ultimate mark or measure or something—of my regard for her: or of her goodness—is a feeling I've had ever since I just knew her: I don't like hurting anyone, but I'd rather hurt anyone else, than her.

In the margin, Agee added: "By 'her' I mean Mia, and I think the bottom of it is that the one thing you can rightly *never* forgive yourself is to hurt or otherwise misuse *genuine* nobility." On the back of the page, the writer further interpreted his understanding of "*genuine* nobility," stating that he and his mistress only possessed "abortive streaks" of that quality. Agee pointed to his guilt and insecurity as he qualified his statement, "This makes it sound, maybe, as if nobility bored me or I preferred ignobility. That's why I said *genuine*. There's nothing about the genuine that bores me, or that I less . . . love and revere. But I do also like messier mixtures, being one myself."[6]

Despite the clearly expressed grief at his seeming inability to forego his extramarital unions, Agee spoke of "great fun with John." He enjoyed the communion which they shared "most in silence but sometimes in talk," during his hospitalization. But what the novelist seemed to be most consoled by was Huston's own lusty, profligate lifestyle. Although it seems obvious that the writer outdid the director at loose living, Agee appeared to be heartened by Huston's confirmation of what he was about: "We arrived, more or less independently, at a same ringing affirmation of the minimal, ineducible [*sic*] rights of a man: That he has the right, even the obligation to write (or other vocational work) . . . even if doing so, shortens his life or kills him on the spot."[7]

The writer's inclination toward a superstitious belief in fate, in the determinism of all things, is evident in a kind of addendum in his

6. *Ibid.*
7. *Ibid.*

letter to the photographer. In what also seems to be further effort to assuage his guilt, Agee suggested that a man is justified in living deeply and passionately because of the temporal quality of life. John Huston did, in fact, agree with the spirit behind the patient's declaration: "I can hear myself uttering some nonsense about doing things in moderation," the director wrote, "like sleeping eight hours every night and smoking say half a pack of cigarettes a day and only having a drink or two before dinner." The director felt such advice obligatory, under the circumstances, but believed it to be basically "nonsense" as Agee did: "He went on nodding until I faltered and finished. Then he smiled his gentle smile and, after a decent interval, changed the subject." In his memoir of their relationship, Huston remembered that the writer made it clear he did not plan to change his life-style following his convalescence. In the director's view, Agee's intention was consistent with his personality: "We who did know him recognize the fact that his body's destruction was implicit in his makeup." [8]

The novelist's January 22, 1951, letter to Evans contained a closing reference to the fact that his copy of *Botteghe Oscure* had just arrived. *The Morning Watch* was first printed by the magazine before it was released in book form by Houghton-Mifflin in April. The novella, when published that spring, elicited mixed reviews, with some critics believing the writer had made a too-studied attempt to do a virtuoso piece. An unsigned *Time* review provides representative comment: "Author Agee falters, clothing the action with symbols for which he furnishes no clear keys." The magazine reviewer found the story line too esoteric, too psychologically obscure: "Agee's final meaning lags somewhere behind, among the Freudian trees." On his initial reading of the work, Robert Fitzgerald was disappointed: "I myself felt my heart sink when I began to read *The Morning Watch*; the writing seemed to me a little showy, though certainly with much to

8. *Ibid.*; Huston, *Agee on Film*, ix–x.

show." He wondered if Agee were losing his irony and his edge, but he eventually qualified his early negative reaction to the novella: "It is pretty clear to me now that he had to go to those lengths of artifice and musical elaboration simply to make the break with journalism decisive." Perhaps the criticism that gets closest to the meaning Agee intended was that of Whittaker Chambers, the writer's colleague at *Time*. Chambers has written of recuperating from his own heart attack in 1955 and reading *Your Own Beloved Sons* by Thomas Anderson. He particularly remembered a scene from this novel set during the Korean War, in which a "bookish" soldier nicknamed "Little John" is reading *The Morning Watch*. A crude noncom grabs the book from the soldier and tries to suggest it is a sex book. After trying to explain, Little John says, "It's about religion, but it's not a religious book." Chambers added, "Yes, that was it, that was absolutely it."⁹

After James Agee's completion of *The Morning Watch* in the spring of 1950, there continued to be indications that the writer was taking an increasingly religious view of himself in the world. Agee was highly conscious of his pattern of spiritual advance and retreat, and wrote to Father Flye in the fall of that year, "I evidently move, as I imagine many people do, in a rough not very predictable cycle, between feeling relatively uninvolved religiously: and very much involved: though I'm not sure that "religiously" is the right word for it: but anyhow a strong sense of being open, aware, concerned, in the ways which are rooted naturally in religion, or in the more serious kinds of poetry or music, or just in a sense of existence" (September 20 [1950] *Letters*, 183–84). The novelist's statement that he was then experiencing "a relatively very full and emotionally rich sense" of feeling religiously involved, prompted him to add, "But at all times I feel sure that my own shapeless personal religious sense, whatever that may be, is deepening and increasing: even the swings away are

9. Agee to Evans [January 22, 1951 (?)], Humanities Research Center; "Richard's Ordeal," *Time*, April 23, 1951, p. 120; Fitzgerald, "A Memoir," 55; Whittaker Chambers, "Agee," in Duncan Norton-Taylor (ed.), *Cold Friday* (New York: Random House, 1964), 270.

less far away from it: keep some kind of relation with it. I wish I were with you and could talk about this" (*Letters*, 184).

The "shapeless personal religious sense" of which Agee wrote had always been, according to those who knew him best, intrinsic to his personality. But a difference between the neophyte artist and the career professional—if we are to judge from the letters—was that Agee in the last years of his life was able to speak more openly about his own spiritual situation. In one sense, the writer expressed in cyclic fashion his need to reestablish himself vis-à-vis the Church that was so formative in his upbringing.

Olivia Wood recalls that she and Agee had a High Anglican wedding and that for the first three years of their marriage were observant Christians in New York City's Saint Luke's parish. Together the couple attended confession, participated in Sunday services, and observed ritual fasts. These practices, however, "wore off after awhile." While the novelist divorced himself early from the orthodoxy of institutional Christianity, he was unable to dismiss its effect upon him or to keep himself from exploring the relationship between his life and theology. Mrs. Wood remembers a brief visit with Agee in 1954, a year before his death, in Greenwich Village. Of that conversation, one remark of her former husband's stood out: "I'm trying to find out what my religion is." Mrs. Wood believes the comment is indicative of the writer's lifelong search, his religion being the all-important element in his quest for selfhood.[10]

Father Flye agrees with Olivia Wood's assessment, of course, and has written that while James Agee felt ultimately unable to accept some doctrinal positions of the Church, that "he had not abjured religion or Christian faith." The priest has stated that Agee "had a humble sense of wonder and reverence before the mysteries of the universe, of existence, of life, of human lives—a religious sense." Robert Coles has commented on the writer's ambivalence, based on the Agee-Flye correspondence: "Drawn to a Christian view of man, he

10. Olivia S. Wood, interview, March 22, 1977.

123

was wary of institutionalized religion; his keen eye for the phony and pretentious never went bad."[11]

While Agee felt himself "very much involved" religiously during the 1950s, his health was steadily deteriorating. He suffered another heart attack in November, brought on by his failure to heed doctors' warnings. Of his condition, he wrote to Father Flye, "I wish I could take it a good deal more seriously" (November 7, 1951, *Letters*, 189). Among the things that prevented him from doing so, he wrote, was the belief that he could "get away" with moderate smoking. Agee also admitted his "whole habit of physical self-indulgence" was a formidable pattern to break. "The only degree of asceticism or even moderation I've ever given a hoot for, let alone tried briefly to practice, has been whatever might sharpen enjoyment." The writer pointed more broadly, however, to the underlying cause for his self-destructive attitude, his "caring much too little whether I live or die" (*Letters*, 189). Agee realized the problems inherent in such a fatalistic stance but could not bear altering his life-style to correct it. In a subsequent letter to Flye the novelist candidly admitted that he could not cope with the pressures burdening him: "I know Mia is in a chronic kind of pain and sadness, in anxiety for me, because of my heart, and my insufficiently careful attention to it. I am out of work and out of money. The most visible and easy amelioration is through alcohol" (*Letters*, November 23 [1950], 197).

As bothered as he was by the worry he caused those around him, and the shame he felt at his own lack of discipline, Agee systematically shortened his life. Several persons have commented on his chronic failure to go to a dentist. Alma Neuman says that the writer's teeth "rotted off," and John Huston remembered that "Jim only went to the dentist to have a tooth pulled, never fixed." Mia Agee partly explains such behavior as owing to Agee's natural romanticism,

11. James H. Flye, "An Article of Faith," *Harvard Advocate*, CV (February, 1972), 22; Robert Coles, "Childhood: James Agee's *A Death in the Family*," *Irony in the Mind's Life* (Charlottesville: University Press of Virginia, 1973), 59.

which left him "strongly disciplined to let himself be programmed by necessities and of external realities."[12]

Yet Agee's inability to adopt the advice of doctors or family members and friends ranging from Mia Agee to Father Flye was linked primarily to his problem with authority. "He didn't want to feel bound by anything," Alma Neuman affirms, "whether it was a marriage, a mother, or the Church." As a natural consequence, then, Agee's need to elicit disapproval from the people whom he loved most provided him with a reservoir of guilt and shame—ingredients seemingly necessary to the functioning of his psyche. Dwight Macdonald has written that such a mentality became a *modus operandi* for the writer: "He would put off work until he got enough behind to feel satisfactorily burdened with guilt." It was basically for this reason that Agee's repeated attempts to end his dissipation met with failure: "He was always full of good intentions for reform and discipline in the wake of a severe setback, but his reforms never lasted very long."[13]

After finishing his Hollywood movie assignments, the novelist moved back to New York in 1952. Realizing that her husband's precarious health would not permit him to walk up the four flights of stairs to their Greenwich Village flat, Mia Agee found a first-floor apartment at 17 King Street. Once established back in the Village, Agee turned to work begun in California—a batch of television scripts on the life of Lincoln. These sequences, commissioned by the Ford Foundation, were to be aired as part of the *Omnibus* series and produced by his college roommate, Robert Saudek. During the next two years, Agee wrote a script for *Noa Noa*, a dramatization based on the diary of Paul Gauguin and a script centered around Davis Grubb's novel, *The Night of the Hunter*.

12. Alma Neuman, interview, March 21, 1977; Huston, *Agee on Film*, x; Mia Agee with Gerald Locklin, "Faint Lines in a Drawing of Jim," in David Madden (ed.), *Remembering James Agee* (Baton Rouge: Louisiana State University Press, 1974), 159.

13. Neuman, interview, March 21, 1977; Dwight Macdonald, "Death of a Poet," *New Yorker*, November 16, 1957, p. 216; Mia Agee, "Faint Lines in a Drawing of Jim," 159.

In February of 1954, Mrs. Flye died and James Agee returned to Saint Andrew's for her funeral. The loss of this woman, whose warm tenderness and mysticism Agee had always deeply loved, was keenly felt. Mrs. Clyde Medford remembers standing outside the Saint Andrew's Chapel, weeping after the services, and Rufus Agee embracing her, saying, "I know just how you feel."[14] In December of that year, Agee wrote to the priest:

> I think I will tell you, my dearest friend; last night I had a dream, during which, in context of general dying (Mia was going to have to die) your wife and my beloved friend, as I arrived at St. Andrew's for her burial, stepped out of her coffin (without stepping back into life) and came towards me up a crowded aisle in the Chapel, and we embraced and kissed as we always have, after a long time apart—as if it were only a few days since we had seen each other. She is among the Saints, and I think she always was. (December 4, 1954, *Letters*, 220–21)

After completing the school year and doing summer duty at Saint Luke's Chapel, Father Flye moved to Wichita, Kansas, to serve as assistant at Saint James' Church.

On September 6 John Alexander Agee, the writer's second son, was born. Concurrent with the arrival of his fourth child, however, the writer's health was still in decline. The early December letter to the priest describing the dream of "general dying" also included himself, as he wrote to Father Flye in the same note: "I've been finding more and more constant awareness of death, and the shortness of time, and of time wasted" (*Letters*, 215–16). Mia Agee believes that Agee did, in fact, have "premonitions of his death." The fibrillations, which he experienced in California, came more frequently and were "painful and scary," according to Mrs. Agee. The novelist kept track of the sequence because he "wanted to see what affected it and what didn't."[15] Agee's letter to Father Flye in late January, 1955, refers to

14. Mrs. Clyde Medford, interview, December 14, 1976.
15. Mia Agee, interview, March 24, 1977.

"as many as 8 [attacks] a day" (January 24 [?], 1955, *Letters*, 221), and a March note speaks of twice that number: "I've been better the past week, in general, than for the two weeks before—dropping, by and large, from an average 12–17 attacks per day, 6–8 of them mild, to an average 6–8, nearly all of them mild" (March 17, 1955, *Letters*, 226).

While Mia Agee says that the writer's recording of his heart spells was the "first real evidence of his taking care of himself," she agrees that her husband "was psychologically incapable of moderation, even during the period of his last illness." Agee's motto, according to his widow, was "a little bit too much is just enough for me." [16] In May, however, Agee seemed to sense that his time had run out. In his last letter to Father Flye, written five days before his death and never mailed, the novelist wrote: "I feel in general, as if I were dying: a terrible slowing-down in all ways, above all in relation to work" ([May 11, 1955], *Letters*, 220).

Certainly throughout his life James Agee was alternately fascinated and horrified by the notion of death. He was preoccupied by the prospect of death in his own life and in his writing. "Death figures in sixteen of Agee's twenty-one known pieces of fiction," Jeanne M. Concannon has stated. "It is treated explicitly in thirty-nine of his one hundred thirty-nine known poems." Previous chapters have discussed Agee's once firmly held belief that he would die at the age his father died. In chapter four, the concept of "magical thinking" was discussed in relation to Rufus' and Catherine's attempts to grasp the meaning of their father's demise. William M. Lamers, Jr., the psychiatrist who has explored this notion in young children, has written of the manifestations of magical thinking in a listing uncannily appropriate to Agee:

"I am responsible for what happened,"
"For punishment, the same thing will happen to me"
(e.g., I will be taken away),

16. *Ibid.*; Mia Agee, "Faint Lines in a Drawing of Jim," 159.

"The same thing will occur to me when I reach the same age at which this happened to my parent."

Normally, Dr. Lamers states, "the magical thinking of childhood gives way to the more conventional thinking of adult life." But for the child deprived of a parent "on a temporary or permanent basis," as in the case of Agee, the psychiatrist suggests that a "psychologic need for parenting" may become so pronounced that such thinking develops into an aberration.[17]

And so with the death wishes and fantasies that so often consumed him, it is with prophetic irony that on May 16th, two days before the anniversary of his father's death thirty-nine years earlier, James Agee suffered a fatal heart attack while riding in a taxicab in New York City. Curiously, too, he was on his way to a doctor's appointment. The writer was pronounced dead on arrival at Roosevelt Hospital. That evening David McDowell telephoned the news to Father Flye, who came from Wichita on the night plane. On Thursday of that week, the priest conducted the funeral service at Saint Luke's Chapel for this one whose friendship had been so sublime, so enduring. Prior to the burial later that day at the Agees' farm at Hillsdale, New York, Father Flye read the Burial Office and conducted a simple Requiem. The priest's meditation was brief and direct: "It is not the custom of this Church to eulogize its dead. I can only say that those who knew James Agee will never forget him."[18]

Essentially because Agee lived by contradictions, the task of assessing his life and career is limited from the outset. As a writer and as a man, he instinctively moved away from labels, from categories, and took delight in bridging genres. Agee was by nature a skeptic, a writer who "didn't trust a book that was a best seller." Dwight Macdonald believes that Agee was destined to be an iconoclast from birth,

17. Jeanne M. Concannon, "The Poetry and Fiction of James Agee: A Critical Analysis," (Ph.D. dissertation, University of Minnesota, 1968), 25; William M. Lamers, Jr., "The Absent Father," in Edward V. Stein (ed.), *Fathering: Fact or Fable?* (Nashville: Abingdon, 1977), 70–71.
18. Flye, "An Article of Faith," 23.

as one "spectacularly born in the wrong time and place." Kenneth
Seib agrees, stating that the writer "is, first of all, essentially a Romantic writer in an age that repudiates Romanticism." Inasmuch as
he was something of an eighteenth-century man of letters, Seib and
Macdonald believe Agee's versatility is disturbing to a modern au-
dience bent on specialization. Because of the variety of genres in
which he worked, Kenneth Seib concludes that "James Agee con-
founds our traditional notions of greatness."[19]

Another critic, W. M. Frohock, has also spoken to this issue—
namely, concentration of effort in a particular field versus working
across the broad spectrum of literature: "Conventionally, if one writes
a book of poems which 'show promise' then one must go and write
another book of poems or the promise is not 'kept.'" Frohock attributes Agee's decision to go against the American literary grain to a
lack of "the traditional respect for genres." Whittaker Chambers con-
curs in Frohock's assessment of the writer's individuality: "He was
savagely unconventional, and, in most practical matters of life, bel-
ligerently irresponsible." Macdonald also finds fault with the writer's
choosing to work in virtually every literary medium: "Although he
achieved much, it was a wasted, and wasteful life." Macdonald has
written with candor and impatience about Agee's diffusion of talent:
"I have always thought of James Agee as the most broadly-gifted
writer of my generation, the only one who, if anyone, might someday
do major work." For Agee's friend that hope was ill-founded: "He
didn't do it, or not much of it, but I am not the only one who expected
he would."[20]

Robert Fitzgerald takes exception to this lament of Agee's mis-
used creative gifts. "Jim may be a Figure for somebody else, he cannot be one for me," the Harvard professor has stated, with obvious

19. Neuman, interview, March 21, 1977; Macdonald, "Death of a Poet," 216; Kenneth
Seib, *James Agee: Promise and Fulfillment* (Pittsburgh: University of Pittsburgh Press, 1968),
129, 1.
20. W. M. Frohock, "James Agee: The Question of Unkept Promise," *Southwest Review*, XLII (Summer, 1957), 223. Chambers, "Agee," 271; Macdonald, "Death of a Poet,"
216, 204.

reference to his close friendship with the writer. "Quite contrary to what has been said about him, he amply fulfilled his promise." Mia Agee defends her husband's multifaceted career on the grounds that financial considerations dictated the writer's *oeuvre*: "He had a great deal of difficulty staying with a thing as long as he liked. . . . he was constantly interrupted by the necessity of earning money." Perhaps the most eloquent testimony in support of Agee's decision to work in a variety of media is John Updike's review of the *Letters of James Agee to Father Flye*. In this provocative essay, "No Use Talking," Updike strongly disagrees with Macdonald's verdict that Agee was mistaken to work for so many years on *Time* and *Fortune*. "Surely a culture is enhanced, rather than disgraced," Updike wrote, "when men of talent and passion undertake anonymous and secondary tasks." Literary reputations, Updike contends are crafted from such "minor" projects. Numerous critics have felt compelled to wonder in print and to puzzle over the question of "What if?" with regard to Agee—a trend that Updike eschews. To Dwight Macdonald's rueful remark that "Like Keats, Agee died when he was beginning to mature as an artist," Updike sensibly argues that it is illegitimate either to speculate on an "unfinished" career or to award fame to a writer for endeavor formerly misunderstood or regarded as "failed" and consummately tragic. On this topic, John Updike crafts his review into a *tour de force*:

> A fever of self-importance is upon American writing. Popular expectations of what literature should provide have risen so high that failure is the only possible success, and pained incapacity the only acceptable proof of sincerity. When ever.in prose has slovenliness been so esteemed, ineptitude so cherished? In the present apocalyptic atmosphere, the loudest sinner is most likely to be saved; Fitzgerald's crack-up is his ticket to Heaven, Salinger's silence his claim on our devotion. The study of literature threatens to become a kind of psychoanalysis of authors. I resist Agee's canonization on these unearthly standards. Authors *should* be honored only for their works. If Agee is to be remembered, it should be for his few, uneven, hard-won suc-

cesses. The author of the best pages of *Let Us Now Praise Famous Men* and *A Death in the Family* owes no apology to posterity.[21]

While I respect Updike's assertion that writers *"should* be honored only for their works," the task of separating the author from the man in the case of James Agee is virtually an impossibility. Louis Kronenberger has written that "all the sympathy, generosity, nobility of feeling that beat through the words shone equally in his actions." For the writer's *Time* colleague, Agee was one of the "painfully few" possessing "great gifts who are even more distinguished as human beings." As has been noted elsewhere, the writer embraced life with a fierce, almost manic energy—whether talking, loving, drinking, smoking, or writing. A co-worker at *Time*, Brad Darrach, recalled the "archetypal scale" on which the writer lived: "Jim once told me he felt as though a high-tension electric cable were running through his chest and that wire had been snapped off and was shooting out tremendous amounts of electricity." Dwight Macdonald has perceptively pointed to Agee's comment on D. W. Griffith's death, stating that the novelist was, in a real sense, speaking autobiographically: "He was at his best just short of his excesses, and he tended in general to work out toward the dangerous edge."[22]

It is perhaps most illuminating that when friends or family members attempt to describe Agee, no one fails to address the centrality of religion in his life and works. Dwight Macdonald has observed that the writer's religion was a unique blend of piety, "irreverence, blasphemy, obscenity, and even Communism (of his own kind)." Whittaker Chambers concurred that the writer "was not a religious man, not in most senses understood by the Westminster Confession, which was Jim's. But he was," Agee's friend at *Time* continued, "among all

21. Fitzgerald, "A Memoir," 57; Mia Agee, quoted in Louise Davis, "Two Deaths in the Family," Nashville *Tennessean*, February 8, 1959, p. 11; John Updike, "No Use Talking," *New Republic*, August 13, 1962, p. 23; Macdonald, "Death of a Poet," 221.

22. Louis Kronenberger, "A Real Bohemian," in David Madden (ed.), *Remembering James Agee*, 112; Brad Darrach, quoted in Alicia Fortinberry, "Let Us Now Remember a Famous Man," *FYI*, February 3, 1975, p. 2; Macdonald, "Death of a Poet," 221.

men I have known—turning them over carefully in my mind—the one who was most 'about religion.'" Chambers' assessment of Agee's religious sense is seconded by Louis Kronenberger. Writing in *No Whippings, No Gold Watches*, Kronenberger has stated that "His 'life,' though unimportant beside his personality and his work, had its standard ingredients of legend-making: there were wine and women in it, and moments of rage, and others that suggested bravura. . . . What perhaps, in the man one knew, provided a resonant inner voice and an added dimension was Jim's religious nature, which ran very deep in him." One of the most telling examples of what has been called the writer's "alive religious nerve," is a recollection by Olivia Wood. She vividly remembers that each time she and Agee left Father Flye's company, the writer would "reverently" ask the priest: "Father, will you give us your blessing?"[23]

In an eloquent, authentic way this simple gesture becomes a metaphor for the writer's life—for his feverish seeking after approval, his wanting benediction before stepping into the world whose pleasures he could not forsake. Mary Haskell could have been writing of James Agee's relationship to James Harold Flye when she recorded in her journal: "People are always longing for someone to help them realize their best selves, to understand their hidden self, to believe in them and demand their best." The writer's search for selfhood was an odyssey characteristic of his own tortured, expansive, oceanic personality, stretching from the Tennessee mountains and Eliot Quadrangle, to a sharecropper's farm in Alabama, to New York and Hollywood. Some have suggested that James Agee never really learned who he was, that his existence remained an enigma to the very end. Mia Agee, while she believes that the writer was always questing for his identity, felt "a line of great consistency running through his life." For her, "He was a person who was always himself."[24]

23. Macdonald, "Death of a Poet," 219; Chambers, "Agee," 271; Louis Kronenberger, *No Whippings, No Gold Watches* (Boston: Little, Brown, 1970), 141; Wood, interview, March 22, 1977.

24. Kahlil Gibran and Mary Haskell, *Beloved Prophet*, ed. Virginia Hilu (New York: Knopf, 1972), 330; Mia Agee, interview, March 24, 1977.

Surely a means by which Agee attempted to explore his interior self was fiction. As noted previously, the rolling head of the father/John the Baptist figure in the "Dream Sequence" for *A Death in the Family* becomes, significantly, "like a Grail." The Rufus figure finds this essence of the man elusive; the severed head temporarily eludes his grasp. Finally, the child-man captures this piece of flesh only when it turns in upon itself. The rolling head—the representation of the search for the father—is analogous to Richard's chapel vision of the Grail and to Agee's own selfhood quest. Each "fact" was finally and irrevocably consumed in anger and love, guilt and joy. In the last days of his life Agee, like Richard, felt "empty and idle," believing "in some way he had failed." Yet, paradoxically, the writer "was also filled to overflowing with a reverent and marveling peace and thankfulness."[25]

In Agee's iconoclastic world there was a fragile wholeness, a coalition of dark furies which moved him on to the next poem, novel, or film script. "A wild yearning violence beat in his blood . . . and just as certainly the steadier pulse of a saint," a friend has written of the tensions pulling within Agee. "He wanted to destroy with his own hands everything in the world, including himself . . . and to worship God, who made all things."[26] The chalice, the Grail that Richard sees in his mind's eye was also the writer's goal: "I'm trying to figure out what my religion is."

That Agee's sought-after Grail was dry and empty is a poignant, fitting symbol for a spirit that raged, flickered, and ultimately burned itself out. In translating the power that was his life into his literary creations, the writer's words were penned in his heart's blood. In the end, as in the beginning, James Agee saved nothing for himself.

25. James Agee, "A Death in the Family" (autograph working draft, in Humanities Research Center, University of Texas at Austin); James Agee, *The Morning Watch* (Boston: Houghton-Mifflin, 1951), 87.
26. T. S. Matthews, "Agee at *Time*," in David Madden (ed.), *Remembering James Agee*, 118.

SELECTED BIBLIOGRAPHY

PRIMARY SOURCES

Books and Articles

Agee, James. *Agee on Film: Reviews and Comments.* New York: McDowell, Obolensky, 1958.

————. *Agee on Film, Volume II: Five Film Scripts.* New York: McDowell, Obolensky, 1960.

————. *The Collected Poems of James Agee.* Edited by Robert Fitzgerald. Boston: Houghton-Mifflin, 1962.

————. *The Collected Short Prose of James Agee.* Edited by Robert Fitzgerald. Boston: Houghton-Mifflin, 1962.

————. *A Death in the Family.* New York: McDowell, Obolensky, 1957.

————. "James by Himself." *Esquire,* LX (December, 1963), 149.

————. *The Letters of James Agee to Father Flye.* New York: George Braziller, 1962.

————. *Let Us Now Praise Famous Men.* Boston: Houghton-Mifflin, 1941.

————. *The Morning Watch.* Boston: Houghton-Mifflin, 1951.

————. *Permit Me Voyage.* New Haven: Yale University Press, 1934.

————. "Religion and the Intellectuals." *Partisan Review,* XVII (February, 1950), 106–113.

Unpublished Manuscripts and Correspondence

Humanities Research Center, The University of Texas at Austin
    Agee, James. Correspondence with Walker Evans, 1936–1951.

SELECTED BIBLIOGRAPHY

————. "A Death in the Family." Autograph working draft ("Dream Sequence").

————. "A Death in the Family." Notes and fragments of manuscript.

————. "A Death in the Family." Notes and manuscript.

————. "Let Us Now Praise Famous Men." Notebook.

————. "Let Us Now Praise Famous Men." Typed and typed carbon copy manuscripts, incomplete.

————. "The Morning Watch." Incomplete manuscript drafts and notes.

Letters from Subject to:

Donaldson, E. Talbot [1932]. In possession of Donaldson.

Macdonald, Dwight, 1927–1938. In possession of Macdonald, New York.

SECONDARY SOURCES

Critical Books and Articles on James Agee

"Agee on Agee." *Newsweek*, July 23, 1962, p. 75.

Agee, Mia, with Gerald Locklin. "Faint Lines in a Drawing of Jim." In David Madden (ed.), *Remembering James Agee*. Baton Rouge: Louisiana State University Press, 1974.

Alpert, Hollis. "The Terror on the River." *Saturday Review*, August 13, 1955, p. 21.

Barson, Alfred. *A Way of Seeing*. Amherst: University of Massachusetts Press, 1968.

Bingham, R. "Short of a Distant Goal." *Reporter*, October 25, 1962, pp. 348–50.

Chambers, Whittaker. "Agee." In Duncan Norton-Taylor (ed.), *Cold Friday*. New York: Random House, 1964, 268–71.

Chase, Richard. "Sense and Sensibility." *Kenyon Review*, XIII (Autumn, 1951), 688–91.

Coles, Robert. "Childhood: James Agee's *A Death in the Family*." *Irony in the Mind's Life*. Charlottesville: University Press of Virginia, 1973.

Concannon, Jeanne M. "The Poetry and Fiction of James Agee: A Critical Analysis." Ph.D. dissertation, University of Minnesota, 1968.

da Ponte, Durant. "James Agee: The Quest for Identity." *Tennessee Studies in Literature*, VIII (Winter, 1963), 25–37.

Davis, Louise. "Two Deaths in the Family." Nashville *Tennessean*, February 8, 1959, pp. 10–11, 20.

————. "He Tortured the Thing He Loved." Nashville *Tennessean*, February 15, 1959, pp. 14–15, 21.

Dardis, Tom. *Some Time in the Sun*. New York: Scribner's, 1976.

Dempsey, David. "Praise of Him Was Posthumous." *Saturday Review*, August 11, 1962, pp. 24–25.

Dunlea, W. "Agee and the Writer's Vocation." *Commonweal*, September 7, 1962, pp. 499–500.

Dupee, F. W. "The Prodigious James Agee." *New Leader*, December 9, 1957, pp. 20–21.

————. *King of the Cats and Other Remarks on Writers and Writing*. New York: Farrar, Straus, and Giroux, 1965.

Elliott, George P. "They're Dead but They Won't Lie Down." *Hudson Review*, XI (Spring, 1958), 131–39.

Evans, Walker. "James Agee in 1936." Foreword, in James Agee, *Let Us Now Praise Famous Men*. Boston: Houghton-Mifflin, 1960.

Fiedler, Leslie. "Encounter with Death." *New Republic*, December 9, 1957, pp. 25–26.

Fields, Pat. "Knoxvillian Nostalgically Recalls Visit with Agee in New York." Knoxville *Journal*, November 2, 1962, p. 8.

Fitzgerald, Robert. "A Memoir." In *The Collected Short Prose of James Agee*. Edited by Robert Fitzgerald. Boston: Houghton-Mifflin, 1962.

Flye, James H. "An Article of Faith." *Harvard Advocate*, CV (February, 1972), 15–17, 24.

————. Introduction to *The Letters of James Agee to Father Flye*. New York: George Braziller, 1962.

Fortinberry, Alicia. "Let Us Now Remember a *Famous Man*," *FYI*, February 3, 1975, p. 2ff.

Frohock, W. M. "James Agee: The Question of Unkept Promise." *Southwest Review*, XLII (Summer, 1957), 221–29.

————. "James Agee—The Question of Wasted Talent." *The Novel of Violence in America*. Boston: Beacon Press, 1964.

Goodman, Paul. Review of *Let Us Now Praise Famous Men*. *Partisan Review*, LX (January, 1942), 86–87.

Gregory, Horace. "The Beginning of Wisdom." *Poetry*, XLVI (April, 1935), 48–51.

Hicks, Granville. "Suffering Face of the Rural South." *Saturday Review*, September 10, 1960, pp. 19–20.

137

SELECTED BIBLIOGRAPHY

Holder, Alan. "Encounter in Alabama: Agee and the Tenant Farmer." *Virginia Quarterly Review*, XLII (Spring, 1966), 189–206.

Huston, John. Foreword to *Agee on Film, Volume II: Five Film Scripts*. New York: McDowell, Obolensky, 1960, ix–x.

"In Love and Anger." *Time*, September 26, 1960, p. 112.

Kauffman, Stanley. "Life in Reviews." *New Republic*, December 1, 1958, pp. 18–19.

Kazin, Alfred. "Good-By to James Agee." *Contemporaries*. Boston: Little, Brown, 1962.

Kramer, Victor. "Agee: A Study of the Poetry, Prose, and Unpublished Manuscript." Ph.D. dissertation, University of Texas, 1966.

————. "Agee's Use of Regional Material in *A Death in the Family*." *Appalachian Journal*, I (Autumn, 1972), 72–80.

————. "James Agee's Unpublished Manuscript and his Emphasis on Religious Emotion in *The Morning Watch*." *Tennessee Studies in Literature*, XVII (1972), 159–64.

Kronenberger, Louis. *No Whippings, No Gold Watches*. Boston: Little, Brown, 1970.

Lakin, R. D. "D. W.'s: The Displaced Writer in America." *Midwest Quarterly*, IV (Summer, 1963), 295–303.

Lamers, William M., Jr. "The Absent Father." In Edward V. Stein, ed. *Fathering: Fact or Fable?* Nashville: Abingdon, 1977.

Larsen, Erling. "Let Us Not Now Praise Ourselves." *Carleton Miscellany*, II (Winter, 1961), 86–96.

Little, Michael Vincent. "Sacramental Realism in James Agee's Major Prose." Ph.D. dissertation, University of Delaware, 1974.

Macdonald, Dwight. "Death of a Poet." *New Yorker*, November 16, 1957, pp. 224–41.

————. "Jim Agee." In David Madden (ed.) *Remembering James Agee*. Baton Rouge: Louisiana State University Press, 1974.

McDowell, David. "The Turning Point." In David Madden (ed.) *Remembering James Agee*. Baton Rouge: Louisiana State University Press, 1974.

Matthews, T. S. "James Agee—Strange and Wonderful." *Saturday Review*, April 16, 1966, pp. 22–23.

————. "Agee at *Time*." In David Madden (ed.) *Remembering James Agee*. Baton Rouge: Louisiana State University Press, 1974.

SELECTED BIBLIOGRAPHY

Mayo, Charles W. "James Agee: His Literary Life and Work." Ph.D. dissertation, George Peabody College, 1969.

Stevenson, David L. "Tender Anguish." *Nation*, December 14, 1957, pp. 460–61.

"Tender Realist." *Time*, November 18, 1957, p. 18.

Trilling, Lionel. "Greatness with One Fault in It." *Kenyon Review*, IV (Winter, 1942), 99–102.

"Unquiet One." *Time*, August 3, 1962, p. 60.

Updike, John. "No Use Talking." *New Republic*, August 13, 1962, pp. 23–24.

Weales, Gerald. "The Accidents of Compassion." *Reporter*, December 12, 1957, pp. 42–43.

———. "The Critic in Love." *Reporter*, December 25, 1958, pp. 38–39.

Wensberg, Erik. "Celebration, Adoration, and Wonder." *Nation*, November 26, 1960, pp. 417–18.

Other Works Cited

James Agee: A Portrait. Caedmon recording (TC 2042). New York: Caedmon Records.

Lathem, Edward Connery, ed. *The Collected Poetry of Robert Frost*. New York: Holt, Rinehart, and Winston, 1969.

Webb, Eugene. *The Dark Dove*. Seattle: University of Washington Press, 1975.

Wolfe, Thomas. *The Story of a Novel*. New York: Scribner's 1936.

Reference Works

Anthony, Sylvia. *The Discovery of Death in Children and After*. New York: Basic Books, 1972.

Bowlby, John. "Childhood Mourning and Its Implications for Psychiatry." *American Journal of Psychiatry*, CXVIII (December, 1961), 481–98.

Brown, Felix. "Depression and Childhood Bereavement." *Journal of Mental Science (British Journal of Psychiatry)*, CVII (July, 1961), 754–77.

———. "Childhood Bereavement and Subsequent Psychiatric Disorder." *British Journal of Psychiatry*, CXII (October, 1966), 1035–1041.

Caplan, Marion G., and Virginia I. Douglas. "Incidence of Parental Loss in Children with Depressed Mood." *Journal of Child Psychology and Psychiatry*, X (December, 1969), 225–32.

Freud, Sigmund. "Mourning and Melancholia," in *The Standard Edition of*

SELECTED BIBLIOGRAPHY

the Complete Psychological Works of Sigmund Freud. Translated and edited by James Strachey. London: Hogarth Press, 1957, XVI, 243–58.

Unpublished Manuscripts and Correspondence

James Agee Memorial Library, St. Andrew's School

Agee, Annabel King. Correspondence with Walter B. Chambers, January 6, 1973.

Fitzgerald, Robert. "Agee Library Dedication Banquet Transcript," October 14, 1972.

Flye, James H. *et al*. "Relationships with Agee," panel discussion transcript, October 14, 1972.

Madden, David. *A Death in the Family* panel discussion transcript, October 13, 1972.

Peyton, William M. Correspondence with Walter B. Chambers, November 29, 1972.

Phillips, Edmund J. Correspondence with Walter B. Chambers [1972].

Reishman, John. *The Morning Watch* panel discussion transcript, October 10, 1972.

Stott, William. *Let Us Now Praise Famous Men* panel discussion transcript, October 12, 1972.

Other Correspondence

Coles, Robert, to the author, April 8, 1977, in possession of the author.

Flye, James H., to the author, August 4, 1977, in possession of the author.

140

INDEX

Agee, Alma Mailman. *See* Neuman, Mrs. Alma

Agee, Emma (sister). *See* Ling, Mrs. Emma Agee (sister)

Agee, Hugh James (father): 1, 2, 3, 34; impact of his death on son, 4, 17, 30, 80, 84, 85, 110, 113, 114, 115; in fiction, 3, 89–100 *passim*, 107, 108, 109

Agee, James Rufus
—early life: cultural heritage, 4, 89, 90, 92; family, 1, 2, 3, 14, 59, 66, 89–114 *passim*; father's death, 4, 7, 9, 17, 29, 30, 79, 80, 84, 95, 96, 97, 98, 103, 108, 115; home life, 3, 4, 10, 14, 20, 32, 35, 81, 89, 90, 92, 94, 107
—youth and education: academic performance, 5, 6, 16, 17, 21, 26; description of, 6, 7, 21, 22, 40, 55, 56, 119, 131; Exeter, 11, 14, 15, 21; friendships, 6, 7, 15, 18, 21, 22; Harvard, 21, 22; intelligence, xiii, 2, 5, 7, 58, 76, 83; need/search for approving earthly/heavenly father, xv, 4, 54, 99, 116; St. Andrew's, 5, 6, 10, 14, 82
—life-style: xiv, 26, 62, 121, 127, 131; bumming, 24; in Florida, 57, 58; in Hollywood, 119, 120, 124; in Nebraska and Kansas, 24; in New York, 55, 56
—personal characteristics: 105, 129; ambivalence, 52, 59, 65, 82, 87, 109, 111; caring and compassion, 6, 22, 40, 41,

43, 45; diversity, xiii, 129, 130; empathy, 40, 41, 42, 43, 67; loneliness, 6, 7, 12, 84, 110, 116; loss of control, 22, 23, 24, 29, 58; need for approval, 40, 105, 106, 116, 132; self-deprecation, 28, 29, 30, 34, 58, 64, 65, 85; sensitivity, 6, 40, 44, 76; sensuality, 24, 48, 49, 50, 51, 52; sexuality, 12, 19, 20, 47, 48, 50, 51, 62, 63, 78, 105, 119, 120
—personal habits: dissipation, 25, 56, 85, 119; drinking, 24, 25, 55, 56, 85; excesses, 85, 119, 127, 131; film aficionado, 21, 117, 118; lack of discipline, 26, 31, 124, 125; poor hygiene, 119, 124; self-indulgence, 85, 124, 132; smoking, 55, 56, 85, 119, 124; talking, 26, 56, 85, 131
—personality, xiv, 32, 68, 131, 132
—relationships: with Dorothy Carr, 15, 18, 19; with editors, 53; with peers, 55, 58, 84; with tenant families, 40, 46, 47, 51, 71; with therapist, 115; with Saunders in-laws, 58, 59, 114; with wives, 31, 57, 58, 60, 62, 63, 65, 68; with women, 10, 14, 20, 56, 62, 132
—significant events: jobs, 26, 27, 66, 68, 118; marriages, xiv, 31, 53, 58, 64, 68; children born, 66, 68, 118, 126; divorces, xiv, 59, 68; health problems, 119, 124, 126; death, 128
—career and creative life: xiv, 25, 27, 31,

141

INDEX

INDEX

—psychological trauma: 7, 10, 23, 31; death of father, 7, 9, 17, 29, 30, 84, 103, 115; mother's remarriage, 14, 15; prospect of divorce, 59; separation from mother, 7, 10, 81, 82

—religious consciousness: xv, 32, 33, 69, 70, 71, 113, 122; awareness of creation, 35, 51, 123; Bible sources, 12, 50, 52; church ritual, 35, 52; theological language, 35, 48–52 *passim*

—religious orientation: doubts, 32, 35, 38, 70, 82, 107, 123, 125; innate, 32, 69, 70, 122, 123, 131, 132; practices, 14, 28, 52, 69, 70, 83, 123, 133; relationship with the Episcopal church, 4, 65, 123; search, 35, 54, 69, 70, 71, 82, 122, 123, 133; training, 13, 63, 71, 123

Agee, Jay (father). *See* Agee, Hugh James (father)

Agee, Laura Whitman Tyler (mother). *See* Wright, Mrs. Laura Agee (mother)

Agee, Mrs. Mia (wife): 69, 119–126 *passim*; quoted, 47, 56, 61, 63, 68, 70, 81, 82, 114, 115, 126, 127, 130, 132

Agee, Rufus. *See* Agee, James Rufus

Agee, Via (wife). *See* Wood, Mrs. Olivia

Agee-Flye correspondence: 11–126 *passim*; confessional nature of letters, 13, 25, 26, 65; openness of letters, 11, 13, 22, 27

Agee-Flye relationship, 5, 6, 10, 15, 17, 32, 38, 65, 70, 73, 78, 79, 128, 132

Alabama tenant assignment, 38–71 *passim*

Alabama tenant families: 38, 39, 46, 47; clothing, 49; housing, 48, 50; labor, 44, 45; life-style, 41, 44, 49

Anna Maria Key, Florida, 36, 38, 57, 58, 61, 114

Bowlby, Dr. John, 8, 9, 29. *See also* Childhood grief theories

Brown, Dr. Felix, 9, 29, 30. *See also* Childhood grief theories

Childhood grief theories: loss/grief/depression cycle, 29; guilt at living, 30, 102, 103; loss/anger/re-

proach/recovery/search, 4, 8, 9, 59, 101, 109, 110, 112; magical thinking, 101, 127, 128; pathogenic mourning, 9, 30; primary separation anxiety, 9

Evans, Walker: quoted, 29, 38, 39, 40, 46; mentioned, 38, 39, 40, 42, 48, 53, 60, 64, 71

Exeter. *See* Phillips Exeter Academy

Flye, Father James Harold: 5, 6, 32, 38; father figure, 7, 10, 11, 32, 79, 114; spiritual father, 4, 12, 32, 79; in writings, 34, 78, 79; quoted and mentioned *passim* throughout

Flye, Mrs. Grace, 7, 34, 38, 73, 126

Fortune (magazine): as employer, 26, 27, 36, 52, 57, 64. *See also* Alabama tenant assignment

Freud, Sigmund, 9, 11, 28, 29, 37, 61, 114

Fritch, Mia. *See* Agee, Mrs. Mia (wife)

Harper, 52, 60, 64, 66

Harvard Advocate: 25, 27; parody of *Time*, 27

Hobson, Wilder, 57

Houghton-Mifflin, 52, 53, 66

Huston, John, 72, 117, 118, 119, 120, 124

Jung, Carl G., 61, 114

Lamers, Dr. William M., Jr.: 101, 127, 128; magical-thinking analogues, 101

Life (magazine), 117

Ling, Mrs. Emma Agee (sister): 5, 7, 8, 91, 101; quoted, 81, 92, 98, 117

Lytle, Andrew, 88

Macdonald, Dwight: 19, 20, 21; quoted, xiii, xiv, 11, 12, 17, 27, 40, 52, 53, 56, 87, 125, 128, 129, 130, 131

McDowell, David: 73, 86, 88, 128; quoted, 5, 10, 12, 14, 16, 17, 40, 62, 73, 74

Mailman, Alma. *See* Neuman, Mrs. Alma

Nation (magazine), 68